Inside
Dance

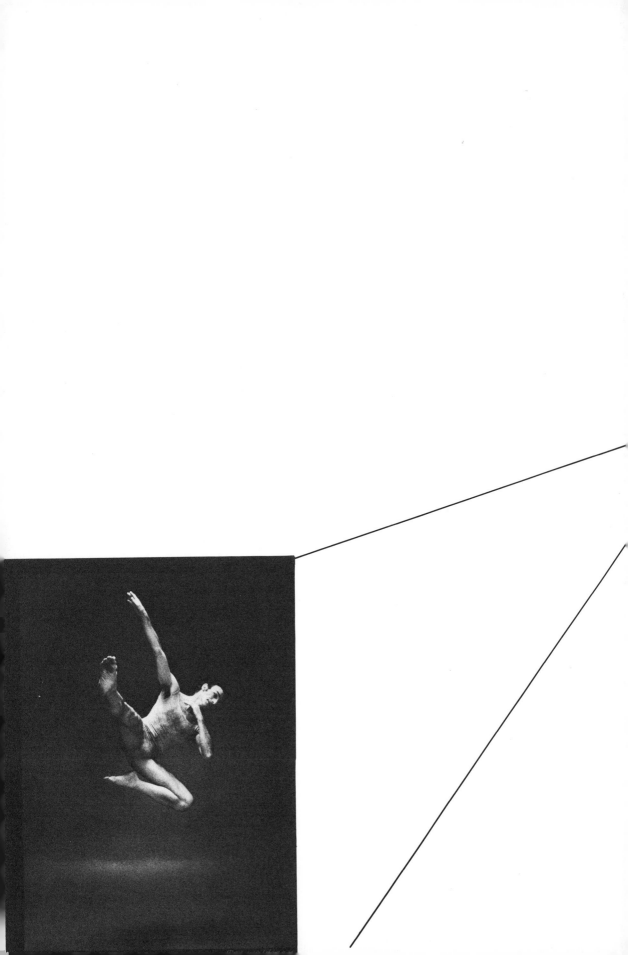

Inside Dance

Essays

MURRAY LOUIS

Foreword by
MARCEL MARCEAU

Introduction by
ALWIN NIKOLAIS

St. Martin's Press

New York

Photo Credits

jacket photo, copyright © Tom Caravaglia
pps. ii, viii, 8, 44, 70, 128, 152, copyright © Max Waldman
p. 4, copyright © M. Billingsley
pps. 22, 108, copyright © David Berlin
p. 28, copyright © Ken Duncan
pps. 36, 90, 116, copyright © Milton Oleaga
p. 52, copyright © Tom Caravaglia
p. 82, copyright © Dan Ziskie
p. 96, copyright © Jack Vartoogian
p. 134, copyright © Ralph Sandler
p. 160, copyright © smb

Note: Portions of the essays have previously appeared in *Dance Magazine* (between June 1976 and January 1978), and are reproduced here with kind permission from Danad Publishing Company, Inc.

Library of Congress Cataloging in Publication Data

Louis, Murray.
  Inside dance.

  1. Dancing.   I. Title.
GV1594.L68   793.3   79–29639
ISBN 0–312–41871–X

Design by Deborah Daly

Contents

Foreword

What can I say more with my poor words than Murray Louis himself about his art? Only that he commands and masters his thoughts as well as his body, and both controls are astonishing. Not only is Murray Louis a master in the craft of modern dance, but also a real Prometheus chained on the ground between sky and Earth, deeply anchored and rooted like a ship sailing through vast oceans—the waves of emotions he stirs through his legs and body are breathtaking, he is dramatic like Duse, witty like Mark Twain. *En Resume* a great dramatic actor and dancer; I would even say mime if it would not make me a little jealous. He is a total artist in the pure sense of the word. I love him because I love the way he has command over his work, and the way he lives and breathes totally for the art. In one word and with many silences on my part, he is one of the few great dancers and choreographers in the history of modern dance. Let me define him at last: he is like Keaton, a master of the absurd dance and choreography ASSOLUTA. The rest is silence.

—Your silent servant
Marcel Marceau

Introduction

Murray Louis has for many years been a major spokesman for his profession—as a dancer. On the international scene critics have acclaimed him as one of the greatest American male dancer-choreographers. Those of us within vocal range also are unmistakeably aware that the richness of his dance artistry has an equally brilliant counterpart in his verbal wit. Given the appropriate moment, his facile tongue will lash like the tail of a tiger, or purr like a kitten; strike with crippling devastation, or lavish love, admiration, and generosity.

His ability as both a dancer and a writer stems from an unquenchable curiosity and an ability to absorb experiences. These in turn ricochet with incredible speed through a high-spirited and multi-channeled mind. In his dancing the results are quick and explosive, entering into a lithe body that immediately quivers like an Aeolian harp to the tune of his heart and soul. This same wit and compassion serves his lips and pen, and this is apparent in this book of essays.

Murray speaks from the inside. He is not a writer who learned about dance. This is a great dancer with a wholehearted affection for his art and for all those who labor with devotion in it. He has often been the Robin Hood, daring to shoot verbal barbs into anyone whom he thinks makes unnecessary misery in the profession, or parasitically elevates themselves at the expense of their fellow artists.

Murray justly calls this book *Inside Dance*. Murray is where the inside is at. He's been there for three decades.

He was brought up in New York City, in the oriental bazaar of the Lower East Side. From Calcutta he once wrote, "I thought I'd be terrified of this country, but somehow it feels like home. It's somewhat like Rivington Street when I was a kid." To Murray, an oriental souk was a variation of his New York scene. At the age of eight he went to live in Brooklyn in a castle-like orphanage, complete with turrets, where he secluded himself in the library with books of every sort. At fourteen he left the castle to spend his time between a pleasant suburban Brooklyn home and the real Bohemia of Greenwich Village with his sister Fran. This was during the W.P.A. days of Federal Theater, the Writers Project, and the period that coincided with the gestation of American Modern Dance. Murray often sat in the wings turning the music pages for Genevieve Pitot as she accompanied Helen Tamaris' eloquent dance passions. Another sister, Ethel, also donned her leotard for classes with Benjamin Zemach. "The city itself was more my home than any home I actually lived in," he said. He lived at the Metropolitan Museum. He saw his first live cow on the fifth floor of Macy's department store. At eighteen he was drafted into the Navy to serve in World War II.

In 1946 he was discharged in California, where he began to dance, write, act, and explore all the prospects San Francisco had to offer a hungry twenty year old. Then, in the summer of 1949, he appeared in my classes at Colorado College. He was a too-slender, but not quite skinny ex-gob, sporting worn-out T-shirts, sailor trousers, and a wide grin that exploded on his face with an ingratiating infectiousness that shattered somber space, and still does. Murray's friendliness is more than warmth; often it's an overwhelming assault.

It was obvious from the start that Murray was of the rare tribe of natural dancers. Upon his return to New York, his development at the Henry Street Playhouse was rapid. He taught the children (we had 400) with a magic the legendary Pied Piper would have envied. He also trained and refined his performing command, and crafted a choreographic style uniquely his own. In just a few short years, *The New York Times* critic, John Martin, singled him out as someone to watch, someone who had in good part arrived artistically. Occasionally Murray dined with Martin, who found Murray's wit and frankness a challenging whetstone to his own. Like most artists, he has a certain wariness of professional criticism; nevertheless, among his closest friends are some of the world's best critics. His chapter on John Martin is a touching and unusual tribute from an artist to a critic.

Murray has left his mark, founded upon a very distinguished career and an unusually warm personality, throughout the professional world of dance. He has as easily won the respect and admiration of a Nureyev or Bruhn, Vassiliev or Marceau, as of the audiences around the world who have witnessed his work. He has struck new ground in his book, and it is perhaps not unreasonable to expect that here, too, he will leave his mark. The joy of these essays is that they are engaging writings from the perspective of an artist. They are personal opinions and accounts accumulated over the many years of his professional life. He writes genuinely and conversationally about a little known but often overly glamorized profession, from the inside—a vantage point too infrequently found in the literature of the dance art.

—Alwin Nikolais

Preface

This book is about dancers. It is also a book for dancers, to assure them they are not alone as they are battered by the exhaustion and the glory of their profession. Teachers and choreographers are also addressed in this collection of essays, because the art is comprised of the intricate symbiosis of the three.

But it is mainly from the dancer's point of view that I have written. I have tried to be verbal in their nonverbal land.

Without dancers there is no profession. No teachers, choreographers, critics, musicals, chorus lines; no dance managers or bookers, no dance boutiques, no "Nutcrackers," no dance anything; because in the beginning there is the dancer and on the seventh day, should he rest, so will the entire profession.

The dance in America is a small profession and, in all honesty, exists through the efforts of about two dozen people. It has not, except in a few cases, institutionalized itself as foreign companies have, in spite of the many outside hands who would seek to force it into that mold. A mold whose icy fingers will inevitably freeze up the frail heat that motivates the frail bodies that comprise the art.

As this profession gets to be more and more unwieldy and complicated, dancers tend to be overlooked. It is their vitality, skill, artistry, hope, need, and endurance that is the very soul of this profession. Yet they are hampered and coerced by finances and opportunity, faced with a national temperament that still views them as extraneous, never relieved of that uphill climb, and once successful pressed over the hill by the squeeze of time. This book is about those who must train and make their art before the specter of maturity claims them, leaving them to their scrap books of reviews and clippings, to faded candid shots and glamorous glossies which stare into the future, fixed, faded, frozen, and forgotten.

Dancers work and live from the inside. They are almost always in pain, physically and mentally. The responsibility of keeping in shape is never ending and crushing. They can never let down. This intensity of behavior, which laymen find trying, is for the dancer essential. They drive themselves constantly, producing a glow that lights not only themselves, but audience after audience. They personify life itself.

They are elegant and strange-looking. Long and short, distinctive and nondescript; generous and selfish, one-tracked and no-tracked. But they know how to come alive like no other creature on earth and live to do so.

On stage they become super-human, which makes it all too easy to forget how human they really are.

Once during the first Grand Tour of Europe I made with the Nikolais Company, a moment of truth occurred which in my thirty years of performing still remains with me most vividly. We began the tour in Venice with great success, and as the company approached Paris, an enormous amount of excitement and anticipation preceded our arrival there. It was opening night and the performance began. The tension grew and grew, the audience breathlessly awaiting each piece. Suddenly I was on stage for my solo. The stillness was frightening. The sound score, filled with silences as well, made the theater's silence even more ominous. I had danced the role many times. I was confident and in good shape, but suddenly, as I prepared for a final movement which went from great speed to a suspension in relevé, I became conscious of how that moment could either bring the evening to a heightened pitch or dampen its momentum. Everything that Nikolais created and everything that had been generated in the audience of fifteen hundred was conduited through me. Everything was riding on the brilliance of that next movement.

My nerve endings reached out to the furthest seat, my muscular system was rooted into the deepest part of the movement, my intellect in control of the phrasing, and my emotional faculties, waiting, glittering in every pore.

"What an incredible responsibility for a human body," I thought. "Here is a physical instrument forced to expand and reach beyond anyone's concept of ability," but, I also thought as I prepared for the step, "You're an artist doing his job." With that, I landed on that leg, held it, turned my head slowly downstage and brought the house down. The rest of the program was clear sailing for me.

Later that night, I tried to put myself in the despairing frame of mind I would have been in had I not brought off that performance. If I had missed or wavered in my footing. Not to be masochistic, but to prepare myself for that day when I *would* miss.

Dancers live on hope. They hope they can get through a performance. Hope they get the job, hope they won't fall off their center when they turn, hope that the studio is warm, hope they get a larger role, hope their practice clothes are dry.

Their needs are simple, their aspirations great. They are also alone too much inside themselves. Pitying themselves, nursing their wounds, hanging on, trying to make sense of the emotional and physical barrage which is always tearing them apart. Their inner roles are not to be envied, regardless of how admired their outer performances may be. All a dancer wants to do is dance. Hand in hand with the glory of achievement rests the terror of getting out of shape. From the magnificent to the mundane.

I wrote this book primarily to give a voice to these nonverbal artists. Teachers talk, choreographers talk, critics talk (and talk), but dancers *do*.

May I propose a toast. "To dancers. For whatever personal hell you may go through. For whatever professional calumny may be heaped upon you. For whatever comfort this may bring, be assured, you are not alone. You *are* the profession. Without you there is no dance."

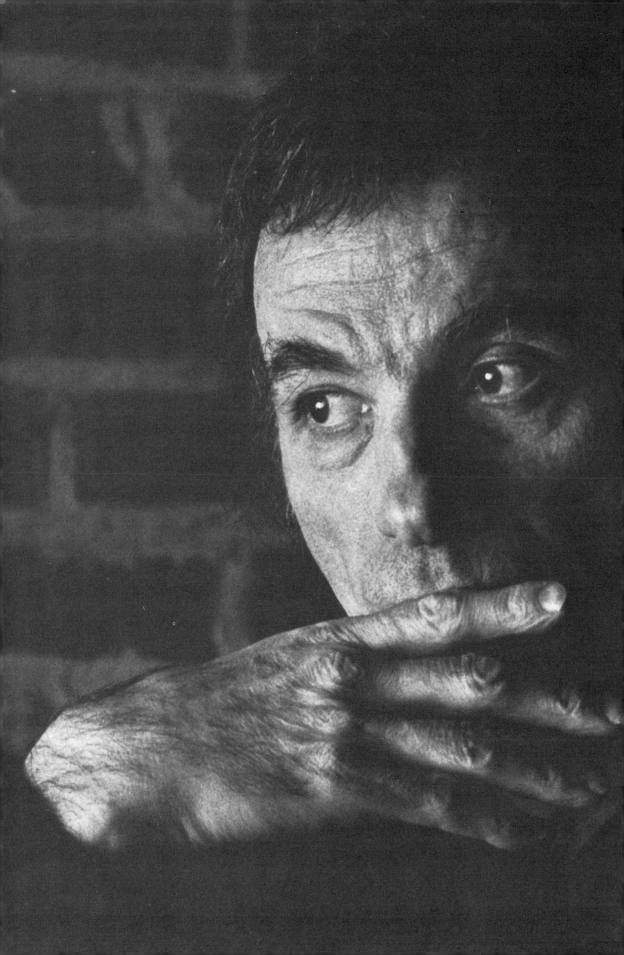

From the Inside

When I was fourteen years old, I saw my first modern dance concert. When I was sixteen, I sat in the wings of the theater and turned pages for a Tamiris concert. When I was twenty-one, I drove with four other people across the country from San Francisco to New London, Connecticut, to see Martha Graham open the Connecticut College Summer Dance Festival, (World War II had just ended). When I was twenty-two, I met Nikolais. When I was twenty-six, or was it twenty-seven or twenty-eight, I made my concert debut, and when I was thirty-two, I felt I had arrived as an artist.

My entire life and career has been dance. Dancer, choreographer, teacher. Nothing has ever diverted me from my passion for this art, and I feel it safe to say nothing will.

I've seen the profession grow, change, define itself, redefine itself, but my perspective has always been from the inside. Earlier, dance had always been a contained art, motivated by a handful of dedicated people. Its problems and jealousies were, in a sense, private, and its successes were grudgingly shared. The people in the profession had a very strong sense of themselves, their work, and their identity. It was not a large community, and left alone it did its work.

I do not wish to imply that this isolation was welcomed. The clamoring for funds, audience, and opportunity was as active then as it is today, with of course one small exception: we had none of those things then and today we have them all. But what also made that period different from today was a germinal difference, an intrinsic difference, a basic difference. Before, the art was shaped and dealt with from within, and today it is being fashioned from without. What constituted the art then was the dancer, the teacher, the choreographer, and the small devoted audiences one managed to attract. These things were within our grasp. Classes, creating, rehearsals, and teaching all occurred within the only security we knew, the studio. Everything made sense in that studio, everything fell apart and came together there.

Artists, performing artists in any case, often referred to the stage as a holy place, a temple; but if the stage was the temple, the studio was the sanctuary, an inner temple apart from the ceremonial ground. We lived in those studios. Our life and our work were one and the same thing. The floors were rubbed smooth with the oil of dancers' bodies. And at night if you listened closely, the anguish of creating sounded suspiciously like sobbing.

What kept "those people" alive was a list of virtues that today sounds almost too embarrassing to list. Certainly today as I attend meetings, I find myself less and less able to recall them: dedication, integrity, belief, moral strength, aesthetic judgment, beauty, conviction, and others that are beginning to be dropped from the vocabulary.

Aside from the impoverishment, the only thing that rocked our boat was the question, "Why do you people do this?" The question never seriously tipped the boat, it just served as a steadying force, because each time we tried to answer it we strengthened our course. There was no need to "sell" our convictions, we were doing it by creating, which was self-explanatory and sufficient, but the impoverishment was real and factual. We could discuss this and point to that.

There were things we needed and things we were told we could get if we formed a strong "front," which we tried to do. I remember the one meeting when Ailey, Taylor, Nikolais, Cunningham, and I met together with our managers. We, the artists, got along famously, while our managers tore each other and the organization apart. Not one of those managers is managing a dance company today. The organization was dissolved and what went on record was that we, the artistic directors, were incapable of any organizational abilities.

The next outside assistance was a great deal more successful and had a profound influence on the profession. It began a period in which "outside" influence, through assistance, and "inside" control, artistically balanced each other and worked. I would chronologically link that golden period to June

Arey's tenure on the National Endowment for the Arts Dance Panel. And then the flood gates opened and *voilà! le deluge!* The profession was inundated.

That which once emanated from within, from the studio, was now pressured from without. Internal Revenue, Non-Profit, National Endowment, Arts Councils, Critics, Management, Boards of Directors, Fund Raising, P.R., Foundations, Booking, Artists-In-Schools, Association of American Dance Companies, Broadway, Unions, Touring, Ballet Companies, Guest Artists, Box Office and on and on. All of these things feeding upon the fragile nucleus.

I am now concerned for the profession. I wonder and shudder as I think, "What if all these 'outside' factions should pull at the same time?" Would the profession, as we know it, pull apart? Thinking back to Europe in the 1930s and how certain political thinking plucked and entirely annihilated the roots of modern dance abroad, could a concerted "outside" pulling do the same in this country? A thought, a possibility? Far-fetched? Who knows? I know what I would like to see.

I feel, however, that the strains are real. The studio is no longer in control. The dancer, teacher, choreographer can no longer call the shots. We have out-priced ourselves and overexpanded the profession too quickly, and the decisions for the remedy are all coming from the "outside."

The studio is still there. It is the source from which it all began, and after my working day with the "outside," after a day of listening to advice with no understanding, I go back to my studio where I understand, from the inside.

New York City

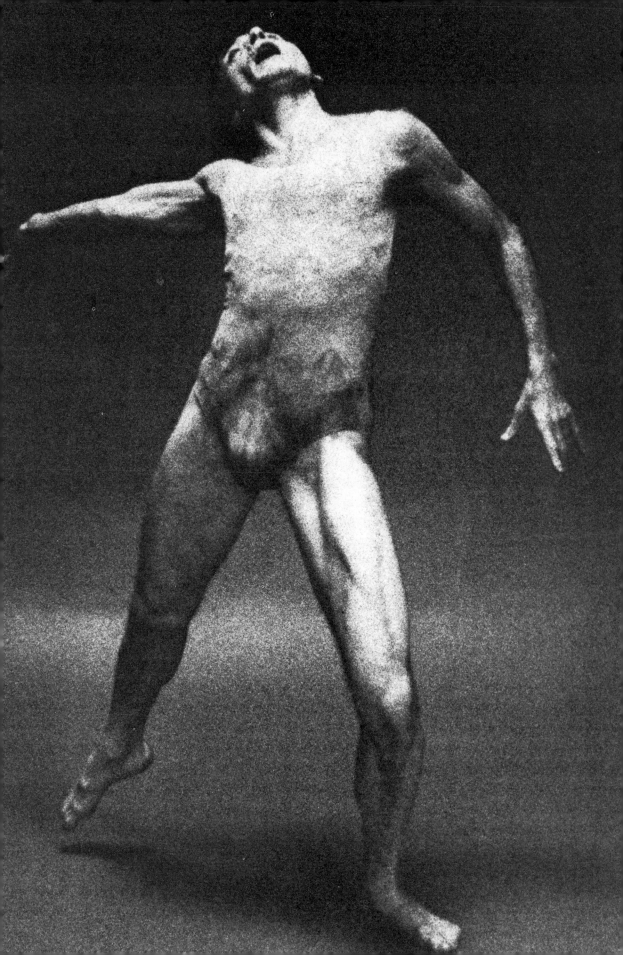

On Sweat

For most people sweating is simply a bodily function that keeps laundries and cleaning stores in business. *Sweaty* is usually synonymous with *soiled.* Sweating is a vastly underrated and generally maligned condition of life, and I'm here to declare, "Sweat is Beautiful."

Firing up the human furnace and bringing to a simmer its large liquid consistency is where it's at.

The dancer works carefully to create a body heat and maintain it throughout a working day. He keeps himself perking with a variety of stimuli. His physical activity is only one of his means to do this. He spikes his day with nerves, tensions, restlessness, anticipation, doubt, and a host of other irritations to keep his body-warmth up.

Heat, or a lack of it, is of primary concern to the dancer.

Air conditioning can strike more terror in a dancer's heart than a slippery floor. An overly heated theater can send his audience off to sleep before the first intermission.

Temperature can call the shots.

From the very first moment the dancer enters the studio to warm-up, the temperature outside and the temperature in the studio will determine the warm-up clothes he'll wear and the speed with which he'll break his first sweat, "open his hips," "stretch his Achilles and hamstrings," and "get his back moving."

Nothing happens with a dancer until he warms up. Pulling a muscle can set him back weeks and breaking a bone can mean months of inactivity. For any other occupation, this recuperative period seems normal enough, but to a dancer it can be frightening and depressing.

A dancer will never "let-go" or "put-out" without first producing an internal heat which will protect his body with the muscular resilience that heat produces.

Generally the warm-up lasts about an hour or an hour and a half every day. The dancer's legendary discipline is based on this warm-up. His grit to get into that studio and do those same damn steps virtually every day of his life verges on the maniacal, and is known as discipline.

In addition to preparing his body, he must also prepare his mind, his psyche. Warming up with a "mad-on" only defeats the purpose of warming up. So that cooling his mind and warming his body is the balance the dancer tries to attain before he rehearses or performs.

It is not a difficult job after a while. Each dancer gets to know himself well enough to create his own formula for preparation, and since very few dancers have the same energy level or time span or stretch or motivation or guts or dedication, it is a small miracle that they can assemble in the same room and, with the same steps, warm-up those highly individual and idiosyncratic instruments, their bodies.

By 11:30 A.M. the dancer has been up for three hours. He has washed, had breakfast, attended to his domestic life for the day, be it as simple as feeding the goldfish, walking the dog, or as difficult as convincing his mate or lover that he has to leave immediately to get to class on time. He then plows through the city traffic, changes clothes, and takes class. Forcing, cajoling, and lying to his body by promising it a long rest in the sun next week, he finally breaks through to that long awaited blessed sweat that says, "Okay, you're ready to dance."

But that is only the beginning. There are still eight hours to span before curtain time. The handling of these hours will separate the student from the professional. The dancer begins the job of pacing himself to maintain his body heat. He must feed his body whatever fuel it needs. From candy bars to nervous energy. He must keep his oven stoked and bank his heat so that his furnace can enflame him during performance.

There are meals to be eaten and naps to be taken during that time, and, when on the road, lighting, staging, and run-throughs to be suffered; the hands of the stage hands to be avoided, dressing rooms to be made habitable, stage and dressing rooms to be heated, tempers to contend with, depressions to elevate, egos to deflate, and bickering to mediate, all washed down with copious quantities of fluids, with and without sugar. Normal run of events for a professional dancer.

The high energy charge before performance is probably the most worrisome level to reach, because once the curtain goes up, the excitement of performance can carry one through. The control maintained during the whole day can now be released. But the hour before performance can be a bitch. Suddenly you feel your legs will not have the energy to get you through the evening. Suddenly you've got to have a ten-minute nap, which is absolutely impossible at that moment. Suddenly your make-up is all wrong, your eyes don't match. Should you take another vitamin B_{12} or gulp down two chocolate bars? If you do any more pliés, you know your legs will buckle, and once down you'll never get up. God! did you leave your performing dance belt in the hotel? No, there it is. Cool it . . . don't cool it. Relax. Don't relax. There's the onstage call. There's the curtain. And there you are. On top of it. Loving it and knowing tonight will be a great performance.

But, on opening nights, energies are not as normal as I just described. In addition, there is the nail-biting terror from the unknown—doubt, whose purpose is to upset the disciplines of the most professional artist.

There are stories about opening nights that are legendary. Wrong sets appearing, blackouts, wrong music, disruptive audiences, artists walking off stage in tears, choreographers fainting, recriminations in the wings—all of which, as you can imagine, makes it very difficult to concentrate on stage, in an already under-rehearsed ballet.

And there is also the reverse of this. The knowing you've got a hit from the first moment on stage and the necessary effort to control that elation.

Martha Graham was a dynamo as a dancer on stage, and she insisted her dancers reach her energy level, as well, before the concert. It is said that one of her devices to stoke up their fire was to make costume adjustments on her dancers just before curtain, like tearing their dresses apart and leaving her dancers to sew them together just before the curtain went up.

With Nikolais, he felt a complete run-through of the entire concert, before the performance, kept our energies up.

How much of this is actually seen from the audience side of the stage? Obviously the people in the first row see the sweat, and those with binoculars often get their lenses sprayed. (Telescopes in the front row have a tendency to throw a little cooling reserve on a fiery performance. It is difficult to project out when your mind strays down to the grooming of your crotch.)

For the most part, sweat creates another dimension of empathy with the audience. An immaculately studied performance can evoke an unnecessary distance between stage and audience, whereas a sweaty, abandoned performance will draw the audience closer, whether they wish to be drawn closer or not.

Sweat can only come from one source, and that is from within, from effort. It is a visual evidence that something is going on, within. Not that what is going on is necessarily good or bad, but at least you know something is going on.

Some dancers sweat more profusely than others. Some dancers finish a performance soaking, their costumes drenched. Foreheads, armpits, backs, chests, discoloring everything that touches them.

But body fluids do not stop there. Noses run, lips get dry, spit accumulates, and these have to be tended to as well.

There isn't any dancer who doesn't know where in his role he can turn his back to the audience so that he can wet his lips, or blow his nose and fling it somewhere.

Tamiris would tell the story of her early days as a chorus-dancing-extra at the Metropolitan Opera House, and of her entrance as an exotic maiden bearing a large cup above her head. On one such performance, Caruso had just cleared his throat and was looking about for a place to spit when he spied this innocent young dancer coming toward him with a cup on her head. She looked at him and he looked at her and as she passed underneath him he let go and hit the cup dead center. It is the closest story I know of a performing baptismal.

I myself have looked at many shocked faces in the wings during my college tours as I solved my runny nose problems on stage.

I wish all my problems could have been so easily solved. One season in New Jersey a particularly bitter, below-zero storm hit the coast. The sponsor in the theater in which we were to perform was reluctant to cancel the show when my stage manager insisted it was too cold. The management called me backstage and turned up all the radiators. Out of one came a stream of water and as it hit the floor it turned, almost immediately, into ice. A sheet of ice a yard square faced us. Reluctantly, he agreed to postpone the concert. Damn finicky dancers, look at all the work we were making for him.

Dancers usually have lean frames. As a result of this, their nerve endings are close to the surface of their skin. They can feel cold acutely. On the first Grand Tour of Europe I did with the Nikolais company, we were on the road for four months. We changed season from summer to fall, and the theaters grew increasingly colder. We performed a great many times and danced every night and rarely were off the stage. Toward the end of the tour we found ourselves in Italy and I had begun to get physically exhausted. The last theaters we played were in Switzerland, I believe, and they were cold. I danced with very little on as a costume and was beginning to grow desperate in my efforts to keep warm. When we arrived in Italy we learned that there was no way to heat theaters and hotels because the heat was obtained from central city-owned sources, and that heat was not turned on until the middle of September. I was frantic. My bones were literally shaking by then and Italy was freezing. The only source of heat was the sun. I took a blanket from my room, went to a park across the street, found a sunny spot where a pony was grazing, wrapped myself in the blanket, lay down, and baked in the sun until I stopped shivering. I never knew what the pony thought, but suspected he would never be caught dead in so foolish a profession as mine where heat was so important and where I pursued a course that always kept me indoors, away from the sun and away from all the thick grass.

Sweating is a natural function of dancers. However beautiful they may appear, however transcending may be their art, sweat will lend its patina to them.

Caracas, Venezuela

On Home

It's 1:00 AM now. From the window of the bus I can see eucalyptus trees and a half-concealed moon. It's the low point of the tour. Energies are low, people are tired, mistakes are happening. Anthony had to set up and do the show without any lighting rehearsal. The equipment arrived at 7:30 tonight. We had to hold the curtain until 10:30 and the audience somehow willingly waited one hour past the normal 9:30 curtain time. We warmed up on a dirty floor of splinters. The stage floor was raked, uneven and a maze of cracks between floor boards, making turns all but impossible. The pressure on my sciatic nerve, which developed a week ago and has been moving from my hip to calf to arch, has now settled into my hip again.

But it is quiet now, as the bus takes us slowly from La Plata to Buenos Aires. There's a great deal of fog out there, and when the moon suddenly appears, I'm in North Carolina where the tall pines paint the same night scene.

Two Tylenol and the cold chicken dinner Helen and Dianne prepared for me to eat on the road have been washed down with half a thermos of hot coffee, and I am lying back in my seat listening to the hum of the bus. It is very quiet, everyone has fallen off to sleep. I get up to put out the reading light over the curled-up form of Sara, settle back in my seat, cover myself with Jorge's sweater, close my eyes, and suddenly I'm home. Warm, fed, tired, and with the family. Together, traveling through the night on a lonely road in Argentina.

What is home when you are away from it half of every year? What aspect of you holds the most vivid picture of it? The image in your mind? The smells, the sounds? The security offered to your vulnerability? People? What?

The moon appears from behind a tree and with what little energy still remains, I laugh, because it is upside down. An upside down moon. I've stared at that same moon in New York, London, Vienna, Athens, Shiraz, Bombay, Honolulu, San Francisco, and Iowa City, but never was it upside down before. But whether it's upside down, sideways or backward, I'd know that moon anywhere. It's the same moon I've talked to since I was a child. It's the same moon I see from my bedroom at home in New York. And there are also the stars. I know them too. When I leave the theater anywhere in the world, I look up at my outdoor ceiling and there they are, my stars, and I'm home.

For the most part, touring is an essential part of the professional American dancer's life. Few companies are theater-based in New York. Few dancers can work predominantly in the cities in which they live. How different from the stifling security of foreign opera houses abroad, where dance is generally part of an established opera society, where dance is an eight-hour job, just one more cog in the whole operation which includes many carpenters, stage hands, and technicians. Everything is prescribed. There is little fluidity, and creativity becomes hampered. But security is assured down to the last fringe benefit and pension. In the U.S., security, with luck, is seasonal. Contracts generally cover the length of run or length of tour. Nothing is assured as far as employment is concerned. Curiously, this unstable climate seems to nurture strong passions, fervor, and a wide range of vivid creative minds. Obviously, both extremes have failings. I hope in my time I can see the necessary balance achieved.

But for now economics means touring, and with one's life so displaced, the dancer must create a living pattern which doesn't drop the thread of continuity and thereby make his life disjointed. He does this by bringing his art ethics into his living ethics.

The subtleties, the imagery, the substitutions, the whole range of artistic translation he practices in performance are now called upon to navigate him through the geographic patchwork of his career. A ceiling at home becomes the sky; an inverted moon, the big dipper; a buttermilk sky in Indiana, moonlight on the Acropolis. There is no interruption. Gulls screaming on Fisherman's Wharf in San Francisco flow into the gliding silent hawks over the Appalachian foothills; the frightening swarms of starlings in Baltimore and the cocky precocious parakeets in a Brazilian bird market are all part of the same aviary.

Who is that coughing? Richard. The cold he contracted in Venezuela has improved, but Peter is also not well. That freezing theater in Curitiba killed him, for that matter it killed us all. He's lost about ten pounds, someone said twenty, as well as his voice.

Everyone else has held up well. The base of this company has been together and touring for five years. Veterans in their twenties. They're frighteningly sophisticated about travel. Among them they speak French, Italian, Spanish, and German; that is, in a manner of very hesitant speaking. But they carry their lives with them. Touring does not break their living processes. Nothing stops. A breakfast of fruit, boiled eggs (four minutes), and coffee is as constant as warm-ups, be it served in a crummy motel on Route 17A on a slushy, dreary winter day just outside of Omaha, or on a balcony overlooking Spoleto on a glorious summer morning.

Spoleto! Spoleto! Spoleto! It was fifteen years ago but how clearly I remember the bathtub episodes. Nick Cernovitch would draw enough hot water and we each had fifteen minutes before the water became too cold to soak in. But it was a big tub and one could stretch out in it. The tub in my apartment was a little sitz bath and the only way I could wash my head and shoulders was to stand upside down in the deepest part of it. I tried that twice and almost drowned. And then someone discovered the shower on the top floor of the theater. It was also the first time I can recall both men and women showering together. We stayed up there endlessly. Finally the stage crew turned off all the lights and went home, and there we were, in darkness, naked, all together in a hot shower in Italy. . . . Ah! Spoleto.

Why have we stopped? The fog? No, I can see animal forms outside. We are on the fringe of the great pampas. No accident I hope. Latin drivers can be harrowing. I can see the animals now. They are cows. Such beautiful animals. I saw my first cow when I was fourteen years old, at Macy's. It was in a farm display on the fifth floor and there was a real cow, standing ten feet from me. It was love at first sight. And those crazy, saucy little goats in India, munching imperiously as the whole world crushes by. Lounging with rakish hauteur. The height of fashion with mascaraed eyes and white-tipped legs. Unhurried, but quick. A satyr's grin paints their mouths. What darlings. But cows and goats are unusual, perhaps not as startling as camels and elephants lumbering down Near Eastern streets, or the lady with her pet ocelot on Hollywood Boulevard, but for a city boy, like me, they are constantly exotic.

The world of animals is really the dogs and cats which exist everywhere.

There is always time to throw a stick for a campus dog, or pause to scratch a kitty behind the left ear. The campus dog is a special breed. Loose-limbed and friendly, relaxed and comfortable. They do more to welcome the frightened freshman and the jaded artist than the cautious handshake and the parrying eye of the administration. They come in all sizes and shapes and some are obviously more literary than others, because I can vividly remember a sign on the library door, somewhere, which read, "Dogs are not permitted in this library." I suppose if a dog can read that sign then there is really no need for him to continue using the library.

Cats, I must confess, are my favorites. I think it is because I do not get embarrassed talking to them as I do talking with dogs and to many people I meet, for that matter. You can pat and thump and ruffle a dog, but a cat you must talk to. I find I can pick up my conversation with each new cat where I left off with the previous one. Cats are wonderful, and I've discovered that despite all their sagacity, they really love to gossip.

Oh! I must stretch my leg. Driving in a bent position for two hours just after a performance is not wise. I'm going to feel this in the morning.

It's sweltering in New York, but winter here. Curious though, there are roses in all the flower stalls. I guess it never freezes here. I wonder what my garden will look like when I return home.

Now I'll stretch the other leg. It's at moments like these, and during pliés, that I'm particularly grateful that the human body has only two legs. But I must admit that while choreographing I sometimes wish there were a third.

Perhaps I'll close my eyes. Careful, if you fall asleep you may be up all night. No chance of that. My sciatic nerve has no intention of letting up. It has settled into a nice little rhythm of pinch, pulse, throb throb throb, pinch, pulse, throb throb, grip. Repeat.

There is one virtue of driving late at night. We are not enveloped in a cloud of carbon monoxide. The whole world is choking itself to death. There is smog everywhere. It is frightening and hopeless. I suppose as long as owning an automobile is the universal measure of achievement, nothing can be done. Traffic is insane in some cities. Once in Athens my driver barely missed an old woman trying to cross the street. In India, I had a driver who hit a child, not seriously, just grazed him, but it took me years to get over that. In Sao Paulo it took forty minutes to travel ten blocks through paralyzing traffic. If you're going by cab through midtown New York during the afternoon, you'd better pack a lunch. Cars have inherited the earth, and the meek shall wait patiently at the curb, forever.

In Teheran you drive wherever there is an open lane. It doesn't matter that it is for traffic going the other way, the path is open, and if you should stop for any reason, you lose the game. Once you get into a cab you could be almost anywhere in the world hurtling toward your destination or your destiny. If I take a cab to a theater, I inevitably arrive a mass of tensions. The trips are usually harrowing. It was only recently that I discovered the defensive system my body could employ. It's called "Close your eyes and don't watch." I find it helps, some.

This driver was specifically told to drive carefully and he has followed orders. He also brought his family to La Plata to see the concert this evening. They are all sitting in the front seats returning with us. That also helps.

The steady hum of the tires is very soothing. Perhaps I should have brought my book. I'm reading Homer's *Odyssey.* In eighteen months I will open a full evening ballet, "Odysseus," with Nureyev as lead, in Vienna. Think of the weight off your back if this were the night after that opening. I'll need two months to rehearse and choreograph it plus keep a harness on Restless Rudi. But if this were the night after opening, I'd be staring into the darkness somewhere, perhaps the moon would be up, drawn into my center, on the edge of sleep, wondering, musing. . . . You're falling asleep.

I wish I'd brought something about Cleopatra to read. That would have made more sense. "Cleopatra" is already in skeleton form. The music has been started, the conception and structure outlined. At the end of August I go to Copenhagen and begin work with the Royal Danish. I look forward to this. Now that I am familiar with the company and the mechanics of the opera house, things will go quickly, or at least quicker.

Don't think about this. Stay in your drowsy stupor. Keep relaxed. Perhaps you should start that new book Ruth gave you before you left. The one about sixteenth century Japan. That's what I'll do. To hell with the *Odyssey,* I'll start a nice luscious novel.

Books are a strong cement in creating a touring-living continuity. Being able to pick up the same book in three different bedrooms every week somehow makes the hundreds of different beds all my own bed. Reading and books are a binding yarn. The more intensely one goes at it, the tighter the weave. There are extremes of course; I know dancers who tour inside a literary cocoon, while others would have trouble making it through an eye examination.

The tourist tries to change as he goes from place to place. Roman in Italy and wanton in Rio, while the professional traveler tries to maintain a constant identity as the scenery and costumes change around him. The tourist returns home and talks about the roles he played, but since the traveler carries his home with him, he has no need to play roles, he weaves everything into his life.

We've stopped again. Now what? We're home. We're here. Oh, getting up. The sins of all my ancestors have fallen upon my legs. It's up to my room. My bedtime ritual. No shower tonight, though. The new book, perhaps I can stay awake to start it. In with my ear plugs, on with my eye shade. Lights out. I reach across the bed, and then the whole bloody game, the whole bloody illusion and half my life comes tumbling down, because the person who should be there is not, and I know where home really is.

Lima, Peru

John Martin

I had a birthday this month. Not an ordinary one, but a major big one, and as a gift, I received from Nik a fantastic present. I haven't any idea who they belonged to originally, but there they were, two volumes of John Martin's reviews from *The New York Times* dating from 1929 to 1938. What a treasure!

The pages are yellowed and the paper fragile and crumbling, but what strength still comes through! Birthdays, as well as rosemary, are for remembrance, and these pages opened more than floodgates to the past and to special memories.

Martin wrote for the *Times* for over thirty years, and when I was a boy *The New York Times* was more than just a newspaper, it *was* New York—and still is for that matter. The *Times* also meant unimpeachable integrity and demanded reverence like the Bible and the dictionary. It was only sufficient to have them in the house and they could ward off all the evils of ignorance, but for a youngster to read any of them was out of the question.

When I was a kid New York was a sunnier place. There were also many more newspapers then, and one associated them with their functional services. The *Times* had the want ads, and the editorials; the *Tribune* the financial page; the *News* had the funnies, or jokes as we called them then, and the gossip. The *Mirror* had the horse racing results. The *Journal American* provided the morning bile, and I never quite knew what characterized the *Herald*.

But on Sundays the *Times* littered the house and I'm sure kept as many families together as did the Church—at least on that day it did. There was something in it for everyone except kids.

The *Times* was respected on every level. Its name was sacred in the city. Even taxi drivers would concede if you quoted the *Times*. It stood to reason to a kid like me that since it was the only paper that didn't carry any funnies, you had to listen to it in the way you did to your grandfather—with awe and respect and absolutely no understanding about what he was talking about.

The period Martin wrote about was before my time; I was growing up then. It wasn't until 1940 that I turned my attention away from my pubic area and began seeing the world around me. By then Martin's scope and singular vision had formed the foundation for the modern dance in America.

Of course, Martin was able to do it only because of the artists who were creating then, and he stumbled as often as they did on their uncharted course. He was learning too. He also found himself entrusted, because of his post on the *Times* and because of his awareness of the great power that that position wielded, with formulating a voice and an audience for an art that usually existed in the papers as a notoriety item, or was covered by whoever was in the press room and unassigned.

If a music critic reviewed, he would shut his eyes and we'd read about the music. If an art critic reviewed, the sets and costumes became prominent, and if the entertainment or sports representative wrote, we'd hear about the girls.

Martin gave the art a voice at a time when it was struggling for articulation. He was every bit as much a pioneer as were the creative artists of that time, and he stuck his neck out as much as they did. He wrote about and dug into the things he saw; he didn't pick at them and he didn't write for himself. He wrote for the art. He knew music and theater. He had his convictions about the social and political scene of the time. He was a philosopher and widely read. He was stoic, witty as hell, droll, and profound.

I was first introduced to John Martin through his books. They clarified and pulled together a great deal for me. It was not until the mid-1950s that I finally met him in person.

Nik had been working for seven years in the direction his art was later to take him, and I felt the work now spoke for itself. We had been pretty much isolated at the Henry Street Playhouse and I thought we were ready for a wider exposure. I called Martin and asked to see him. He arranged for a meeting at the *Times*. I don't know if those little cubbies off the reception room on the second or third floor still exist, but we met there and talked over a bare wooden table, like visiting day at Sing Sing.

I really cannot remember what I said, but I must have been convincing, or else he was being very sympathetic, but he agreed to visit the Playhouse. The following week he and his wife, Louise, appeared at the school and for three days watched classes, listened and attended rehearsals, and then he wrote. It never dawned upon him that he would be "influenced" if he heard the artist present his working process. After all, who knows more about the intent of one's art than the artist? Inarticulate as the artist may be, he is still creating the work and usually knows what it is about.

That was my first meeting.

The second time we met was after a performance. I had just composed "Journal." It was a long forty-minute work. I was then thirty-two years old and finally in command of myself. On that opening night everything worked. I knew who I was and where I was going. When the curtain came down, I walked in a daze of self-realization toward the wings. Nik was standing there and I walked toward him. Suddenly the fire doors clanged open and there stood John Martin. "I must run," he said, and he hugged me and left. I can't remember what else he said because at that moment what I needed more than anything else in the world was to be held, and of all people, it was John Martin who did it. Will I ever forget that man? Never.

Oh, he had enemies, make no mistake about that. Lots of people hated him. Then again, Martin himself had few chosen friends in the profession— yet many people in the profession could call him friend.

In going through the scrapbooks, I found a letter from Lincoln Kirstein. As I read it, I could hear Kirstein's teeth gritting as he tried to remain calm and not antagonize *The New York Times,* whose support he needed desperately for his new Balanchine company. There was no love lost between those two men for a long time. Later on Martin wrote some brilliant and perceptive articles on Balanchine and the wound was patched, but I don't think it was ever healed.

I remember going with Martin to see "Agon" just after it premiered and how irritated he was with how the dancers performed it. They were adding too much of their own personality to the roles. He said Balanchine was critical of this too. I took Nik to see "Agon" and he, too, thought the dancers intruded on the choreography. I couldn't understand how these three guys, independently of each other, had the same reaction while I thought the dancers made the ballet. They were strong personality dancers then—clever, witty and hip, and they brought the piece to life. Today much of what those dancers added is part of the choreography of "Agon." So much for you three guys.

I think about this many times as I struggle with dancers to "give" themselves to the choreography and not just do it as steps.

Dancers are the dance. After all, what is this art but one long continuing path, its frail thread handed from dancer to dancer, leading us all through the labyrinth. The thread is passed along from the passionate to the passionate, from the heart to the heart. The dance is a fire, fueled by everyone touched with the madness of dance, not by those who are drawn to the light, but by those who go mad from the heat and who burn. Martin knew this difference of those who are drawn and those who are burned. He called it passion, and to those who knew this wry, austere Scotsman, passion did not come disguised as passionate indulgence, but was the closest the flesh could come to divinity.

The birthday-present scrapbooks are filled with fascinating names: Graham, Weidman, Tamaris, Humphrey, Wigman, Angna Enters, Holm, de Mille, Massine, Escudaro, Irma Duncan, Kreutzberg, St. Denis, Swan, Mei Lan-fang, Shankar, La Argentina and so many more.

In 1930 he wrote, "Indeed, to be frank, the immediate future of the dance unquestionably lies on this side of the Atlantic, and New York can in all fairness be considered even now the capital, though not the metropolis of the dance world."

Martin had a theory about feet. "You could tell who was a dancer by their feet. By the way they placed their weight upon the stage," he wrote. I remember smiling inwardly as I thought about my own bandaged, split, torn, calloused, swollen, and very tired feet, stuffed into a pair of shoes that I was trying discreetly to remove under a long tablecloth at the French restaurant where we were having lunch one day. But sometime afterward, while rehearsing, I discovered my feet articulating more fully than before. My instep and relevé suddenly went further and I realized that my feet had an appetite of their own to flex and extend and reach for the floor and grip and talk. I knew then that my feet had finally joined my body, that I could talk through them.

He thought Wigman and Argentina had beautiful feet. I couldn't imagine a greater contrast than these two artists. One impeccably shod and the other with gnarled bare feet, but he could see and he saw them all. He also saw Isadora. When I learned this, I made him answer a question which I felt he could.

I had been at a dinner at the home of George Constant, the painter, and another guest was present who had seen Isadora in Boston. He described a dance she did where from a low position she rose up and lifted her arms. He said he had wept.

Two weeks later in the country, at dinner, Natasha Brown spoke of Isadora. "You know," she said, "I saw Isadora in New York and I remember so well one dance where she was on the ground and slowly she rose and lifted her arms and I just wept."

"Tell me," I asked John, "Did you see Isadora perform a dance where she was low on the ground and slowly got up and raised her arms?"

"Yes," he said.

"What was so special about it?"

"I don't know. I couldn't see," he said. "My eyes were filled with tears."

The scrapbooks cover the depression years, a staggering social and economic time for America. Yet while his writing is tinged and colored with the influence this turmoil had upon the dance scene, the account has a timelessness about it. He was able to see through so much and put his finger on what counted. Dancing, choreography, notation, Federal support, the creative artist, teaching, ethnic dance, ballet, visiting artists. He traveled and covered other cities, the stage, films, ice skating, tumbling, summer sessions, legal battles to allow Sunday performances in New York, a new vocabulary for dance, musical forms, and theatrical forms. He ranged over the entire scene wherever dance, or what was pertinent to dance, occurred. But, above all, what was most obvious then was the single-mindedness he evidenced to establish the American modern dance, and at the close of 1938 there was as much dance in the city as there is today, if not more.

He thought the Jooss ballets great, and important, particularly "The Green Table." I saw him last year at the Joffrey Ballet. "The Green Table" was on the program. He asked me what I thought of it. I told him I thought it was great. Had I seen it done by the Jooss company, he asked. No, this was the first time. He looked at me and his face said so much.

I went backstage afterward to see Lisa Bradley and Jooss was there. I was introduced to Jooss. We found ourselves alone and I told him how much I enjoyed his ballet. "Ah," he sighed, "it is so difficult." He gave me the same look as Martin had.

I know what the look meant and what they are both looking for and I also know that no one will ever see those ballets performed that special way again. The Parthenon will never be built again, nor will Chartres Cathedral, but they are still with us. Those ten years of the birth of modern dance will never appear again—that pungency, that lust, that vigor, that rage to move—but they are still with us. One has to have the courage to go back into the labyrinth and find the thread wherever it has been dropped and pick it up again . . . to burn and not simply to look at the flame.

Copenhagen, Denmark

Premiere

premiere ... Webster's definition ... vt, 2: for the first time ...
premiere ... Choreographer's definition ... vt,1: for the last time ...

It's over now, and the cast of characters shall go nameless. Just as well, since I've already called them every name in the book. This wasn't a difficult delivery. I've had worse.

Getting a piece on the boards differs with every choreographer. Our work habits differ, the pressures we need differ, but the agony I'm sure is the same. Choreography is not a sporadic art. The skills and methods of practice are developed through steady pursuit. The theory that after a performing career one will become a choreographer is naïve. The steps of creating structure are practiced as steadily as the steps of dancing. The habits of choreography become as innate to the body as the turnout is to the legs.

Not only are the choreographic processes part of the game, but the necessary collaborations and the hassles they produce also contribute to the way the game is played.

I began the new dance five months before it was first performed. With my schedule, time is invaluable and my need for it often desperate.

I work in a number of ways, but primarily I choreograph the dance first and have the music written afterward. Every dance has its own identity and therefore its own structure. This process allows me complete freedom, particularly in plotting the time structure of the piece. When I work with an already composed score, I select the music for its contributing character to the idea or premise I am working with and then put it aside. I begin composing with no adherence to the music other than its pulse. Only after long phrases of dance are completed do I rehearse it with the music. Since the music generally can't be altered, I make all necessary adjustments to the dance structure. When the entire work is done, then I relate the two and work on the piece as a whole.

I create a minimum of about one hour of choreography a year. This can realize itself as three twenty-minute works, one full-evening piece, or two thirty- or forty-minute pieces. There are some years when I do more and some less. My determining factor is time. As my life gets more complex and so much of the energy goes into survival chores, I am faced with the serious question, "When do I get time to work?"

When I began choreographing for my company, about twenty years ago, there seemed no end to my freedom of subject choice, and Lord knows, I had plenty of time. With luck I could perform my work three or four times a year.

I choreographed all sorts of dances, used all sorts of accompaniment. I tried then, as now, not to allow myself to fall into any single identifiable style of movement, and as a result tried to arrive at as rich and varied a movement vocabulary as I could possibly achieve. If there is any credo I proclaim for myself, it is to let the dance identify itself and, with my skills, bring it to fruition. "Where does it want to go?" I ask and then take it there. I don't always like where it takes me, but I go with it nevertheless.

I begin a dance with a general premise, and then take off. When I reach an impasse, I stop, re-affirm my premise, and go back to where I deviated from it and continue again. I welcome these deviations because they are often the seeds for future dances.

For a given dance, a movement may be wrong. For another dance, that same movement may be perfect. I also don't go along with movements that are harmful to the body and jeopardize the dancer—but that's just a personal quirk.

I've composed many dances over the years and I try honestly not to repeat myself. I've composed psychological dances, dramatic dances, funny ones, satires, lyric, poetic, abstract, *et cetera*, all with the intent of not allowing myself to fall into a restricting and identifiable "style." I don't know why I do this; I suppose it is my nature and as a result has become part of my creative credo.

Over the past few years I have discovered that "other considerations" have begun to flavor my thinking. Balancing the program, challenging members of the company, excluding myself from all new works, and expanding the repertory with octets for the new company size.

And so the general format for the new piece defined itself. 1. It was to be an up-closer. 2. It would be an octet. 3. Since there was a musical commission involved, composed music was to be considered.

And so I started the piece while the company was in New York, and I was free. Free that is with only the normal daily three-hour teaching schedule, an ongoing search for a new manager, a monumental cash-flow crisis to keep Chimera and its complement of forty full-time employees afloat, Nikolais inaccessible on a Far-Eastern tour, and a steady gnawing concern about maintaining my own performing technique. You know, free.

I began to work and the dance took the shape of a five-part suite. I worked in silence as I usually do, accompanying the dancers on drums—which I play reasonably well—during the run-throughs. But the piece needed music desperately, because the drums were locking the dynamics into a steady persistent pulse, and the piece was losing its sweep. "Don't worry about that, the music will take care of it," I told myself.

I was going to call the piece "5 dances," "5 etudes," "Smart Ass Dances," "Encounters," "Glancings," "Glance Encounters," "Glances."

If it was to be "Glances," I had to point it up more, and so four interludes were added using glances and looks to set up each section. It seemed to work, but now the choice of sound was crucial.

"What about lights, Murray?"

"What lights?" "The lighting?" "Oh, the lighting." The lighting I needed to worry about like I needed a hole in the head. Music, that's what I needed, music . . . and the right music, and right now.

So I sat down with Tony (Tony Micocci, my manager) and we went over the piece for its lighting possibilities. I had ended each section with a "period" that took the form of a duet shape. We decided to photograph those shapes and project them at the end of each piece, then cross fade to an abstract slide during the interludes.

"If you're going to photograph them, what are the costumes going to be?"

"Costumes?" God, didn't anyone understand I needed MUSIC?

We settled on simple peacock-colored costumes, because the other two ballets on the program were in white and orange.

Now back to the music.

In the early 1970s, when we were located at the Space, a great group of musicians worked together there and called themselves Free Life Communications. I had just finished "Personnae," I was looking for a composer, and they seemed like naturals. They were primarily instrumentalists and dazzling improvisationalists. Many of them were products of Juilliard and Manhattan Schools of Music and had sound classical backgrounds. But above all they were free thinking, and made terrific music together.

We settled on eight instruments and began our sessions together. On the first day the dancers marked through the dance and the musicians watched, played along, and in general everyone got to know each other. At the end of the first day, we settled on the instrumentation for each section and the general qualities for each dance. They came with curiously naïve ideas about dance accompaniment but by the end of the first session they understood that what I required was their skill in making fine sound. The second day the sessions were great. On the third we met in the recording studio. Two-thirds of the recording room was set up and miked for the musicians. The rest was left open so that the dancers could quietly mark through the dance. The musicians improvised the entire piece. There were six sections in the dance and for three of them we kept the first take. They were fine musicians and they gave me a great score.

I used this technique with a number of other dances and had planned to do the same with "Glances," but the commission stated that the piece was to be played live. The director, administrating the commission, said he wanted to find a new Stravinsky. I assured him that I also cherished that dream.

And the search began. The new free sound I wanted couldn't be written, only improvised and I had to set my head thinking in another direction. In all, I listened to the works of twenty-nine composers. They covered a wide range of approach. It was a great education for me; I learned a great deal about contemporary music.

I don't recall now how Dave Brubeck's name came into the picture but I latched onto it as soon as it was suggested. Brubeck was called and he liked the idea. Dave and Darius Brubeck came a week later to see the ballet. His enthusiasm was infectious, and he said he had the first movement sketched before he left the studio.

As both Brubeck and I were to leave on lengthy tours, it would not be possible to work together. I video-taped the dance to a drum accompaniment and sent it along, together with a count and rhythmic score to Brubeck. Dave could work now with instant rehearsals, and I left with the company for South America.

July 24: I arrived back in the United States for performances and part of a summer session in St. Louis. A cassette of the music arrived, and the dancers and I listened avidly. It was only a piano rehearsal recording but it gave us an idea of the general quality. The tempo of the last movement was too slow. When Dave called from Los Angeles he was pleased and relieved that the last movement could be played faster. Darius, in New York, felt that I needed an overture and some music for the interludes. Darius was off to his first rehearsal with the musicians. Some of them.

August 1: I arrived back in New York. I was home two hours when Jerry called from the Beacon Theater. Would I come there immediately? Nikolais had fainted and was hemorrhaging profusely. (God, as I write this I find myself trembling all over again.) I told him to get Nik to Beth Israel Hospital, that I would have our doctor there, and I would meet him at the emergency entrance.

Nik was conscious and in good spirits when he arrived. Dr. Rosenfeld arrived almost immediately. They put Nik into Intensive Care and put four pints of blood back into him.

How negligible all my problems seemed. Nik was opening with his own premiere in two days and it got to him, the hypertension.

By that evening the bleeding had stopped. There was no ulcer, no need for an operation. Everything was all right. I had to leave the hospital at 10:00 P.M.

August 2: Up at 8:00 A.M. to get ready to teach 104 students at the studio. Our summer session was in full swing, and with Nik out I had additional teaching. Fabulous kids, great energy, and great level. After five hours of technique, improvisation and composition, I staggered to my office and fell asleep at my desk. Over to the hospital. Nik still bleeding but vastly improved. Nothing to worry about. Then up to the Beacon for lighting.

August 3: Teaching, hospital, Nik's opening.

August 4: Teaching, hospital, Nik's second premiere. Then to the Met to see Nureyev in the Schumann pieces. Picked up at the stage door and driven to Connecticut College, arriving at 3:00 AM.

August 5: Today I would hear the score for the first time. Full rehearsal, dancers and musicians at 10:00 A.M. I woke at 8:00 A.M. and tore from my guest cubicle suite to the dining room for breakfast. Breakfast ended at 8:30 A.M. and I missed it. But the coffee machine was there—all was not lost.

I finished my coffee, went to the main office to get a key to get back into my room, as I was told to do by the night guard who opened my door. No key. Would I wait at the door, someone would be there shortly to let me in. 9:30 A.M. The key could not be found. The guard who was called could not get the door open. 9:45 A.M. I could not be late for that rehearsal, and all my things were in the room. At 10:00 A.M. someone found the key. The walk to the rehearsal studio was literally across the campus, another fifteen minutes.

I knew that I was coming into the stretch, because now anything that took time was becoming exaggerated, and getting to me.

When we met, I discovered that this was also the first meeting and rehearsal for all the musicians. The first morning rehearsal was spent limping through the score.

Dave arrived for the afternoon rehearsal, and I began to hear things in the music. The musicians rehearsed very late that day, and I realized I was never going to get the chance to polish the dance before we opened, nor really hear the music. Dave had to leave again and would return for the second night.

August 6: A good run-through in the morning. We also lit the piece. At lunch I was furious at the screw-up with the P.R. and listened to everyone blame the other guy. 8:00 P.M. curtain. Nancy Meehan's company opened the program. The company danced beautifully, what a treat. "Glances" closed the program and fell apart. Half the notes just weren't played, but the dancers got through it.

I called the musicians together after the performance and did some strong criticizing and arranged for an early rehearsal the next day.

August 7: "Glances" played its second performance and everything went well. I was pleased, Dave was pleased, the dancers and musicians were pleased.

"Glances," Opus 70, Choreography by Murray Louis, Music by Dave and Darius Brubeck was born at Connecticut College on August 6, 1976. God, have I gone through this seventy times?

New London, Connecticut

On Critics

The dancer is a vulnerable person. The instrument he employs in his art also serves him in the hassle of his daily living. An upset stomach can jeopardize balance and a heavy heart doesn't help much in getting off the ground. To protect himself, he creates a complex series of insulating devices—a survival manual: he watches the food he eats, takes care of his legs, rests, and builds an immunity against critics.

Since a dancer, when he performs, is a sitting duck, he presents himself as an irresistible target to anyone who cares to snipe at him, and buckshot in print or otherwise is not pleasant.

I have had more than fifty opening nights. Fifty days of dread. Not the normal apprehension of my performance or of the work, but of the crap I would have to read the next morning.

It took me some time into my career to develop my defenses against the press. At one point I asked the press not to come; they were welcome—if they did not review. Most of them accepted their tickets on that basis—and proceeded to review anyway. It wasn't until I hit upon a simple fact of life and nature that relief came. As I walked down the three flights of stairs from my loft on opening day, I would say to myself, "Remember! In twelve hours you are going to be walking up these stairs and life will go on. No one can interfere with that order of your existence." I found that if you survived it, you could learn a great deal from experience. I have had over the years, of necessity, to develop a system to cope with whatever has been written about me. Both the good and the bad, because both have to be guarded against equally.

I try as much as possible to read the stuff when I am sufficiently removed from the event. I can say categorically that nothing anyone has ever written about me has ever influenced my work one iota; but personally, I have responded to the insults, the maligning, the hurt, as well as the elation.

It is this personal maligning that one has to protect oneself against, because that can interfere with the quality of performance. Even if critics aren't, dancers are vulnerable, susceptible. A critic has nothing at stake when he writes slanderously except his success in forming a *bon mot.*

For most dancers, a critic is good if he writes well about them and bad if he writes adversely. A perfectly reasonable evaluation, since that is the way one judges tomatoes. They are either rotten or firm. That's the jungle code of the market place.

In the 1950s and 1960s, when I was evolving my art, I was blessed and frustrated by the limited press opportunities available to the profession. Blessed because I now realize how disastrous it could have been, since I had not as yet developed my immunity to criticism; frustrated because it could have created a momentary spurt to my ego and economics, which is always nice.

It takes time to make an artist. Time to work, to germinate, and to find an identity. The dance is a temporal art, not like painting. A painter's work can outlast a dozen critics, but a dancer has only so many years to make and state his case. Critics will not have this, because most of them are committed to the new, the news, the trendy, and their own egos. There is a particularly appalling trend today among critics to create their own hype, their own image at the expense of the dance art. Most of them will admit this. It is a little like the pressure in academia toward "publishing" that has soured and drained so many good teaching minds. Several have told me directly, "I write for myself." "Who then," I wonder, "writes for the art?"

Most critics are tidy souls. I suppose it's because they sit before a typewriter, which is neatly laid out before them, each letter in place. And once a critic has you categorized, nothing will shake him from his cliché; he'll sink his teeth into it with a tenacity that would shatter a mastiff's jaw. As Alistair Cooke wrote in his book, *Six Men,* "The truth is that the constant viewer is usually prejudiced about the performer before the performance. If he likes you, he will like you all the more; if he dislikes you, he will dislike you all the more."

Many years ago at Connecticut College, a critics' panel was held. At the end, I asked one lady with particularly Freudian views if she would ever retract a statement. "Of course," she answered indignantly, "If I feel I've been mistaken." "Have you ever?" I asked. "No!" she said, implying she was never wrong. Who's never wrong? Lord! A choreographer asks himself nothing but, "Is this right?" or, "Is this wrong?" How is it that critics know what is right and wrong, and once knowing it why are they writing? Shouldn't they be creating or at least be President? The world needs them.

And then there is all that verbiage—all that sheer, exhausting verbiage. Critics using the artist as a springboard for their innermost confessions. Perhaps some kind soul could send them diaries and relieve us of the embarrassment of prying, because whether they realize it or not, they are revealing a part of themselves that a public should not be called upon to share.

Critics usually write about their feelings and ignore the intent of the choreographer, and are generally incapable of dealing with choreographic structure. I have taught and watched thousands of improvisation classes and thousands of composition classes over the years, and I cringe at the arrogance and inadequacy of the dance press regarding choreography. The press today has had a considerable hand in aborting the developments in the field. Critics hover over the creative pasture waiting like the early bird, anxious for the head of any little creative worm to break the ground. Then down they swoop and tug and tug until they succeed in pulling their victim out of his germinal bed and out of all proportion.

This is one of the reasons there is no dance avant-garde today. The tremendous proliferation of critics will not give the avant-garde a chance to nurture and mature. A robin must eat his weight in worms to make his deadline. The avant-garde usually arises when the social fabric of a society is plowed up by some sort of upheaval; economics, politics, war, and revolution help break up the old thinking. There have been three concurrent social revolutions recently: the Black revolution, the feminist movement, and pot. The Black revolution has created a separatist art, the feminists have placed heavy emphasis on gender, and pot has identified itself with a spaced-out concept of time. On the dance scene, the reverberations of the 1950s and 1960s are breaking the most original ground in the 1970s. Perhaps, in the great cycle of things, the swing today is not toward the avant-garde. Bach and Mozart were not of the avant-garde; they followed one. Similarly, we seem to be bringing to fruition the breakthroughs of an earlier, seminal period.

Since there is such a rash of critics around, perhaps critics should review critics. It might get them off the backs of young dancers. It would also balance the odds a little, since the critic has the space and vocabulary to answer his critics; the dancer usually has neither of these. The dancer stands vulnerable, focusing upon creating his art on the one hand, and trying to defend himself on the other. The dancer is helpless to any bully with a byline. There is no reason why criticism cannot and should not be a constructive, positive, and knowledgeable responsibility on the part of people who write about dance. When I conduct composition classes, I criticize the work—not the person. That is my responsibility. I don't behave childishly and call the dancers names; name-calling will never be a substitute for true criticism.

A recent review in a reputable weekly magazine described one of the world's greatest artists—a woman of extraordinary talent and a prima ballerina of a major ballet company—in terms such as "bedraggled," "homeliness," "chinless," "pigeon-breasted," and "bottom-heavy." God! I don't think there was a single dancer who didn't groan to see his profession so vandalized.

The type of critic that disturbs me most is the self-appointed evangelist. Obsessed and abusive, shrill and heedless, seeing only what they wish to see. Summarily dismissing artists out of hand. Arriving at concerts with reluctant sensibilities and looking for any reason to justify their hostility. What in the world is the point of such bitterness? What purpose does calumny serve, and what place has it in art criticism? Why must there be *"The greatest," "The only"*? Which art is comprised of one artist? When critics establish an exclusivity for the art it is dangerous. And when those same critics are placed on Federal dance panels to allocate public monies, it is dishonest.

I believe that criticism in any of the arts must deal with several sensibilities: the sensibilities of the artist, the audience, the circumstances of performance, the reviewer, and the art itself. The critic's role stands as a link between the nonverbal event and the verbal translation for those who have not participated in the experience. That narrow link must at all costs be kept open, clear, and resonant. It must stand free from the blockage of personal biases and the instinct to preach.

The range of dance as it exists today is overwhelming. To cope with it does indeed place an awesome responsibility on anyone's perceptions. It is all the more reason why critics dealing with dance as an art form must learn how to change the filters to their senses with great frequency. Nothing distorts a review so much as one seen through a fogged aesthetic basis. Nor should the residues of previous viewings be carried over to a new event.

If critics wrote about critics, it would be very healthy for their profession. It would be interesting to see what sort of immunity they have developed against their own virulence. The function of critics is multiple: they can fill houses, assuage egos, and when they know whereof they speak, speak it; but to be malicious—never. That's for gossip columnists. Critics can print and run. They offer no means for their targets to retaliate, and for some inexplicable reason, they also think themselves above criticism. There seems to be a gentlemen's agreement in the profession that one critic shall not discuss another.

The people who write about dance in New York City have divided themselves into several camps, with a leader at the head of each and a singular point of view as a focus. Holding allegiance to a single branch of the profession reflects a critic's shortsightedness, especially when in their earnestness to eliminate the other limbs, they chop wantonly at the roots of the art itself. Only artists can be so singularly focused; they need that intensity to see their path. Critics must have a large overview of the scene.

Some of the camps have entrenched themselves more rigidly than others —they are led by cult mothers and served by fluttering votaries: they have dedicated themselves to their narrow vision of the profession and do not hesitate to lay waste to the very art they should be serving, so consumed are they with themselves. Unfortunately, they have taken to presenting their criteria to novices, at courses in dance criticism held throughout the country.

Inconceivable as it may be, there has not been an effective champion for a non-ballet-based dance art since John Martin, and modern dance has suffered for it. It could very well face annihilation if certain critics have their way.

I won't discuss the miracle of critics who arrive drunk and sleep through a performance, and yet manage to meet their deadline.

I won't discuss editors who don't cover events because they are disturbed by the works of a particular artist, creating a censorship which is deplorable in a free press.

I won't discuss the manner in which history, and historical fact, is tampered with and arrogantly distorted.

I won't discuss efforts to upset the ecology, the delicate balance of this profession with attempts to direct the art itself, all of which are daily occurrences.

I also don't feel that an artist should accept criticism from a critic, unless that critic has also given that artist the credit he is due.

I don't think audiences are to be ignored either. When they are roused to cheering and ovations, something must have happened. Yet, I have left theaters with audiences tearing the roof down, only to read grudging sourness in the morning press. I suppose that when one shuts his eyes, his ears turn off as well.

It is evident that the field of critical appraisal must cover the areas of aesthetics, history, reportage, and evaluation. Not many people can fulfill all of these roles. Why do most critics assume they can? I think this is where the problem arises; these areas are not seen and addressed separately. The assumption that all critics know what they are talking about is equivalent to the doomed assumption that all dancers can choreograph, or that all dancers can teach.

Having toured internationally for many years, I am always amazed how critics suddenly get blind spots and won't recognize the different sensibilities to be found in different countries. Instead they gang up on a foreign artist and jump and dump upon him. It is as if they all have to taste blood—a chance to sling their recent accumulations of arrows. This year Balanchine got it in London and Béjart and Neimeirer got it in New York. It was not so much what was written but how it was written that was inexcusable.

Directing myself now to the editors of the press: you allow a great injustice and incalculable harm to a helpless profession. This field does not have the money or the clout that the film industry or the Broadway theater can employ to sway you. We come armed with only the vulnerable integrity an artist can muster. If editors really had the balls, they would open up the game to include the victims, and I don't mean the little playpen called "Letters to the Editor." I mean a new, lusty Elizabethan sport called "Critic-Baiting."

Critics could learn from listening to their "victims." They might even get involved with the art and not write so much in the heat of their heat, not create and use personal definitions of the art before they discover how the working artist and teacher are using the dance vocabulary. And who knows, they might even develop a broader vision of the art, maybe see it from the other side.

To those critics who couch their prose in positive terms, you have my thanks and admiration. But to those who write with malice and insult and are guilty of self-aggrandizement and self-indulgence, I've got something else for you.

New York City

On Classicism
and Style

During the hey-day of modern dance at Bennington College in the 1930s, the boundaries between ballet and modern dance were very clear, mostly because neither knew very much about the other, and each had a very clear stereotype in mind of what the other was: the ballet dancer danced on her toes and danced about swans and princesses, and the modern dancer flexed her bare foot and was always in torment about something, and the men on both sides were generally more supportive than dominant.

The two styles almost never came in contact with each other. By nature, psychology, and predilections, the dancers who participated in either style felt that the other "world" was alien. They turned their natural criticism upon themselves. The ballet people argued Vaganova versus Cecchetti, the French School versus the Russian, while the moderns were "talking" either Graham or Holm, and accepting Humphrey's compatability with Weidman.

Bennington in the late 1930s had brought together the moderns for teaching as well as for performing, and through this competition (and it was competitive, sometimes viciously so), began to define two directions. One direction had to do with classical principles of movement, and the other with a personal movement style of an overwhelming and consuming nature. As with the psychological mentors each prescribed to, the break was clear—one was Jungian and the other Freudian.

By 1941, Hanya Holm and Martha Graham were on two very different paths, one dealing with the philosophy and principles of classicism and the other with a personal style that led to a personal classicism.

Shortly after this, American Ballet Theatre would come into gorgeous blossom, and Lincoln Kirstein and Balanchine would begin their partnership.

What finally brought the two factions, ballet and modern dance, smack into each other was a third form of dance and the dancers themselves. It was a catalyst more powerful than Hollywood, more magnetic than the Met. It was Broadway, and it was triggered off by a loner, Agnes de Mille. She was a loner in her vision and in her art, in her motivations and in her intelligence. She had seen Graham and she had no barriers.

After de Mille's "Oklahoma!" opened on Broadway, and its success was ensured, all the dance barriers came down. Show dancing, later to be called "jazz," joined ballet and modern to become a huge melting pot, serving up whatever a Broadway show might need.

What Broadway really meant was jobs and money. What else do dancers want and need to do more than anything else in the world than dance? And if there was money involved, why, that was so much extra gravy! This is their greatest vulnerability, and the reason why dancers are so weak at the bargaining table—they've got to dance, and those bastards "negotiating" across that table know it.

There were jobs available by the early 1940s. Dancing work. Not for two concerts a season, but for months, maybe years. Look at "Oklahoma!" It was never going to close. And look at the choreographers doing the shows: Robbins, Kidd, Holm and Tamiris, in addition to de Mille.

A tide of all sorts of dancers washed from studio to studio and it was fabulous. I die thinking back just to the "look" of each class. Just a few years prior to all this, the fashion for the modern dancer was black leotard, black jersey, ankle-length skirt and pony-tails for the ladies, and the gentlemen wore pants and skivvy shirts. But now there were colored leotards, tights, mesh hose, ballet shoes, a million different hair styles, short skirts, bosoms oozing out of blouses, French-cut leotards, and men had bulges where they were supposed to have bulges. It was wild! And the teachers were thrown for a loop. "What the hell did all these people want?" Well, let me tell you. What they wanted was *steps*. Steps and routines to make those bloody auditions. All those "artistic" choreographers wanted more than tits and ass.

Nobody knew what was going on, and nobody cared. The war ended and

GIs could study at any accredited school, and men flocked to the dance studios on the ANTA (American National Theater and Academy) list.

The Broadway musical began its climb to the heights it reached mostly through the great dancing on the stage. Broadway was the winner from the first explosion that this dance interaction produced. Ballet Theatre was next.

When the excitement settled down and the hysteria of Broadway abated the modern and ballet dancers, having had to rub noses with each other forcibly, had a chance now to see each other with a more serious and sharper perspective.

Hanya Holm was no longer dancing herself, and because of economic pressure, could no longer maintain her company, but still continued an important school. Her energies were now divided between teaching and Broadway choreography.

Graham herself did not participate in choreographing for Broadway at this time, but many of her dancers did appear in leading roles. She, though, was performing brilliantly and had an impressive company of stunning dancers. She was also into her great period of Freudian-Greek dances.

To the new and curious ballet audience and critics who came to see what modern dance was all about, the modern dance was clearly represented by Graham, by her subject matter, and by her movement style. Holm had by now formulated a concept of classical principles, and Graham had evolved a style that could sear people to their seats.

Teaching is not a glamorous job; it does not stir multitudes. Performing is and does. Many saw Graham; relatively few studied with Holm. Graham's exposure and press was considerable; Holm's was limited.

By 1950, the definition of modern dance was Graham.

By 1950, the definition of ballet was "classical."

By 1980, it is time we redefined definitions.

When the Greeks gave birth to what we know as classical, it was based on balanced proportion, the creation of a structure that gave the finished form a fulfilled identity and life. A visible harmony. But they only dealt with realism, as did the Renaissance and every major period through the nineteenth century.

In the twentieth century, abstraction was born, and in the 1920s "abstraction" was accepted as a concept. But to find the structure and balance that could reveal the identity of the non-real required another rafter of sensibilities, and the dance, like painting, began its search for a new articulation of principles —principles that would reveal the nature of identity in non-literal terms. This identity was essential in order to communicate to an audience. It told the dancer, as well as the audience, what was going on within a movement.

It was probably some art historian, critic, or writer who first used the term "classical" to indicate a chronological demarcation in art history and by doing so created the great confusion associated with the word. By doing so he divorced it from its original meaning. Classical as a standard of criteria does not have its original meaning when it is applied to a period of time. "Classical," "impressionist," "expressionist," "modern," "contemporary" are a matter of history not quality. Time slots for the reference book.

The ballet, primarily a nineteenth century form housed in the traditions of the European opera houses, responded to the three things the operatic form demanded. The first and most important thing was the music. Second, the plots of both the operas and ballets of that time served merely as a framework on which to hang the great arias and dance variations. And third, it was the stars who drew the audiences in. The diva could be counted upon to stop the show with a G above high C, and the *assoluta* was guaranteed adoring applause for her thirty-two *fouettes*.

The ballet vocabulary and form became rigid and locked in, not necessarily because of what was being choreographed, but because of what was taught in the classrooms. The repetition of certain patterns, in a certain way, to certain music, with a certain attitude made the dancers inflexible to anything other than what they were taught. How could they possibly deal with new music when all they practiced to was Chopin? How could they round their backs when they were taught to hold them straight?

If the choreographer and his dancers were not associated with a school that prepared them both in a common vocabulary, he then had to go along with the steps the dancer knew. The choreographer had to use the characterizations the dancers could perform, because there was never time enough for them both to know each other and try new things. Because time was always pressing he tried as much as possible to use dancers with whom he had worked before. Since there was no growth from the inside of the technique, "the new" was tacked onto the outside; new music, new decor and new stars. And when a movement is not brought to its fulfillment from the inside, one is left with only the outer identity, which through repetition becomes a highly developed style, eventually lifeless and only a symbol of dance.

Which brings us back again to the 1950s.

Ballet was at a breaking point. The once dazzling Ballet Russe was in its death throes; uprooted by revolution and war, without a focus, broke, touring itself to death, and held together by the now-frail de Cuevas's hands. And then it just disappeared, somewhere out there.

In America the ballet companies were now demanding a wider range of movement from their dancers. However, the ballet classrooms still provided only the traditional steps, which left modern dance and jazz to provide the other stuff. Once again the ballet growth was tacked on from the outside.

Any technique that teaches certain movements to be performed in a certain way is a style technique. It is easy for anyone trained in a style to copy another style. A little flexed foot here, a little contraction there, a little turn-in here, and *voilà!* Instant modern. The same can be said for the other side; a few extra turns here, a few beats there, an attitude here, and again, instant ballet —hardly classical dance.

But a new classicism had been developing in America. Hanya Holm had done some amazing things; they were rarely realized on stage, so that not many saw them, but they were there. Nikolais saw and picked up that singular, frail thread and wove a basis for a new classicism in dance. He had to isolate himself to do this, because so much was unformed, so much ground had to be prepared, and it had to begin in the studio, in the classroom, and from the inside.

Now anyone seeing Nik's work on stage will say "What the hell are you talking about? The man is a media man. What's this about classicism? You can hardly see the dancer sometimes." True, sometimes. But this is one of the tributes to his teaching. In class he teaches a classic technique. On stage he goes where his vision leads him. His teaching is universal; his art is his own. I won't go into any verbalization about this technique now, except to say that it deals with the skill of identifying and realizing the nature of movement abstraction, which is what dance is primarily about.

Although the dancer becomes an artist on stage, he prepares himself in the classroom for his art. Ballet training needs an overhauling, a re-evaluation and a re-structuring. There is no reason why ballet should become a museum art or hide from the twentieth century behind its "classical" style. We know a great deal more about movement today, but the ballet training as a whole does not employ these new insights. The vitality and life of the twentieth century must imbue its nineteenth century basis. Perhaps in this way the "classical dance" can get back on the road to true classicism.

When modern dance-trained choreographers are engaged to set works on ballet-trained companies, the difficulties are unimaginable. There are two directions to take. The choreographer can work with the ballet vocabulary, or he can fulfill the real purpose of his engagement, which is to extend the ballet dancer's movement range. To do this he becomes a teacher, a villain, a seducer, a tyrant; anything to incite new vision and range.

If by some extraordinary luck the choreographer manages to mount a work upon a company, the vitality and quality of the piece will shine through for a season. Once the piece goes into repertory, it begins to slip back into "balleticism," because that is what is drilled into the dancer every morning in class. Turns and beats. Routine repetition of the routine. The practice of a dry skill which eventually becomes a boundary for limitation.

The classroom should develop within the dancer an ability to taste the kernels of movement as well as to practice the shells. There is no reason why a *port de bras* cannot be practiced as a spatial investigation as well as an arm framing the body.

There is really no such thing as a "classical" ballet today. The carelessness of revivals over the decades and the updating processes of different companies often make some versions of the "classics" unrecognizable. In other arts the materials used to create those arts are also alive, changing only in patina: gold, marble, wood, pigments. But dancers unfortunately perish, and new ones are needed to recreate a work. There is no possible way for a dancer today to perform as his ancestors did. Life makes this impossible; both dancers and audiences grow and change, and despite the efforts of elite scholars, there is nothing anyone can do about it. Even in Russia, where the dancers are bound by hermetically-sealed aesthetics, the restrictions are stifling for the artists, and they are forced to flee before they are crushed by the pressure.

If bodies change, if mentalities change, if cultures change, then why don't the classrooms reflect this growth?

Modern dance has considerably expanded the range and understanding of dance movement. The activation of space in and around the body, the extension of time sensation, the vitality of dynamics; these are only a few of the many things that could be brought into the ballet classroom without disturbing the traditional vocabulary. It is limiting and unrealistic to everyone involved to teach the ballet vocabulary as it was practiced in the nineteenth century. The piano has long since replaced the harpsichord. The issue then becomes, in both ballet and modern dance, a matter of which comes first, stylistic mannerism or classical richness?

Modern dance has also become codified in its definitions and techniques. It is so easy to teach empty mannerisms, styles, and skills. It is very difficult to awaken dancers and insist upon fulfillment of execution, the investing of movement with its full quality and inherent nature. Space, time, textures, and dynamics are part of everything.

Fortunately, there will always be those great artists who are performing in both idioms. They rise above it all. They are those gorgeous few at whom everyone points and says, "That's what it is all about."

It boils down to a simple choice. Either a dancer works toward the routine gesturing that hides the nature of movement, or toward classicism as the Greeks intended it: to reveal the art.

Copenhagen, Denmark

On Eating

For some reason I have always felt the art most akin to dancing is cooking. In thinking it out it is because both deal so vitally with the principle of time —when you make the gesture, when you stir the pot. Cooking is like performing —you can't repeat or correct once the heat is on. Both are immediate arts.

Eating is only second to warming-up in a dancer's day, and with so few hours in that day, he sets up as automatic a pattern for food as he sets up for his stretches. A dancer is an aesthetic machine and only the right food can make that machine operate properly.

Basically, the normal body needs a certain number of nutrients taken in certain quantities in order to function effectively. These nutrients can be ingested in all sorts of tasty disguises. They can also be consumed in quantities totally out of proportion to their need and servicibility. The catch here is the word *normal.* The dancer does not operate a normal body. Everything he does is in excess, both in eating and in living. The demands he makes upon himself are abnormal compared to the layman, and the energy he needs to drive himself as he does comes from the food he eats. His tenacity is fed from psychological sources that are often beyond his grasp, but food he can control.

All dancers will agree that food is essential. The disagreements rest in what the food should be. Nureyev lives on red meat; Anne McLeod is practically herbivorous.

A dancer is very consistent in his allegiances. He will swear the same devotion to each new diet he undertakes. He'll offer himself as living proof that his current nutrients work—that is, until they don't work. Then he becomes an authority on their failure.

Since food becomes such a personal matter and eating away from home has become so impersonal, dancers, like hermit crabs, have taken to carrying a bit of their home with them when they go touring—their kitchens. A great many of the grains and nonadditive foods popular in today's diet are not available or else difficult to find "out there," and as a result dancers travel laden like pack horses. Usually, the smaller the dancer the bigger the pack. Suzie McDermaid (5'1" or 2") carries a bag one-half her weight and one-third her size. She could single-handedly kill chivalry. No one, but no one, would offer to carry her bag.

There are two critical meals for a dancer: breakfast and the performance meal. Breakfast is obviously the first meal after awakening. But the performance meal is tricky. Some dancers can eat a large meal before performing and need to do so, while others must eat after performance. For myself, 5:00 P.M. is the absolute latest I can put anything into my stomach, other than chocolate. I wouldn't get ill if I ate later; I would simply fall asleep. I feed on my adrenaline the hour before performance. Over a period of time the digestive clocks become fairly patterned, and disruptive 10:00 P.M. Latin curtain times are heralded by howling hunger pains.

For me, matinées don't count. I'm never awake until they're over anyway.

Another similarity between dancing and food is that theaters and restaurants have similar working hours. The curtain generally comes down on both at 10:30 P.M. This is disastrous for ravenous dancers after a show, and on many an occasion no laughing matter. My salutation to a sponsor often goes: "Where can we eat after the performance? How are you?" It's simply a matter of first things first.

Away from a very large city, good restaurants never seem to be open late, but someone always seems to remember "someplace out on the highway that usually stays open." And, "No, they have never eaten there themselves, but it's very popular for pizza and stuff like that." And, "I'll give you directions how to get out there; maybe someone in the crew can give you a lift; I'm not sure if the taxis run this late."

Breakfast finds the company drifting into the dining room at various times and in various moods. Surly, bright, sullen, friendly but always a little numb, which is the up-rooting characteristic of the touring syndrome. There is always a degree of apprehension before ordering. The communal survey is made. "Don't order this, order that," "They don't have honey," "The orange juice is fresh," or "Watch Murray's face when he drinks his coffee." If anyone's eye is open in the morning it's the waitress's.

Confronting a dance company in the morning would alarm anyone, and irritated dancers, if they are ever courteous, are certainly not tactful then. Of course, a professional waitress can handle anyone, even to the extent of making you believe there's no such thing as fresh grapefruit in Florida and Bilge's grape water, since that is all they carry, is just as good for you. But there is always the assurance of eggs. I mean what can you possibly do to ruin a boiled egg? Granted it's likely to be served to you cooked anywhere from thirty seconds to twenty minutes; it still has not come in contact with the greasy griddle. There are also those dancers with suicidal instincts who wolf down stacks of wheat-cakes, sausage, fried eggs, heavily buttered toast and everything anyone else has left uneaten.

Dieting does not necessarily have to do with losing weight. It can also mean gaining it or maintaining it. A diet can also deal with maintaining an energy and metabolic level. Dancers with low energy have as much to worry about as those who are overweight. A great deal of both are conditioned by food as well as frame of mind. More should be written about the psychology of eating.

Waves of fasting and cleansing the body periodically sweep a company, often because of the way we feel about food. I remember after the first four weeks of touring India, I became a vegetarian. Not only could I not touch meat, I couldn't look at it on the table. I had three more weeks of touring and I was certain I would get run down and lose weight, which I could not afford, but I was in such good spirits on that tour that I remained perfectly healthy. And that, mind you, was without fresh milk or salads. I tried to continue that diet when I returned to the U.S., but abstinence made the heart grow fonder, and I was soon back to eating all the garbage I ate before. Muscles not only have a mind of their own, but they can also talk. They tell you when they need sugar or salt or rest. Doctors call this talk symptoms; dancers call it cramping up.

There are a number of good things about food and eating on tour. I was over thirty when I visited France for the first time and discovered tomatoes. I'd eaten them all my life but I had never tasted one before. That was momentous for me. Or the time in Bellingham, Washington, when I heaped my plate at a smorgasbord table, and discovered, as I ate, ambrosia. In the Northwest it is called fresh salmon.

The closest I had ever come to Kentucky Fried Chicken was in an elevator with The Colonel himself in Salt Lake City. But once, after a concert in a town so remote I can hardly remember its name, there was no place to eat. Abandoned after the concert by a gracious host, the company had a picnic in the largest motel room. It consisted of Kentucky Fried Chicken and anything else anyone had to eat. We dined while watching a late movie with Bette Davis. I had seen the film thirty years before and remembered it vividly. I had a great time eating that tasty chicken and ruining the film for everyone by anticipating all of Miss Davis's best lines. Ah, the sophisticated pleasures of dining abroad.

However, there are buried across this country some very fine eating places. I don't mean the expensive, big city Fried and Frozen Rooms, but great home cooking places. They have to be ferreted out. Sponsors are reluctant to suggest them because, as everyone knows, artists from New York are accustomed to dining at the Four Seasons and 21, but I've had some great meals in, among other places, Orono, Maine; St. Joseph, Minnesota; Santa Marie, California; Durham, N.C., and as I mentioned, Bellingham. I have also had the most harrowing culinary experience of my life in Chicasha, Oklahoma, where everything, and I mean everything on the table was batter fried.

Taken as a whole, apart from the cooking done in the home, America has a long way to go in its culinary evolution. Nik and I disagree about the root of civilization. He says it has to do with cooking; I say it has to do with hot water. But we both agree that to a large extent the root of *gastronomique* in America is unfortunately, still, gas.

Unfortunately, I am not a great cook. Although I enjoy good food, I'll stop eating anywhere in a dinner when I'm full. I never overeat, but I'm an appreciative eater. Good eaters are essential to the world of *haute cuisine*. You cannot have a fine cook without people who enjoy his cooking. The same could be said for dancers and dancing.

Chicago, Illinois

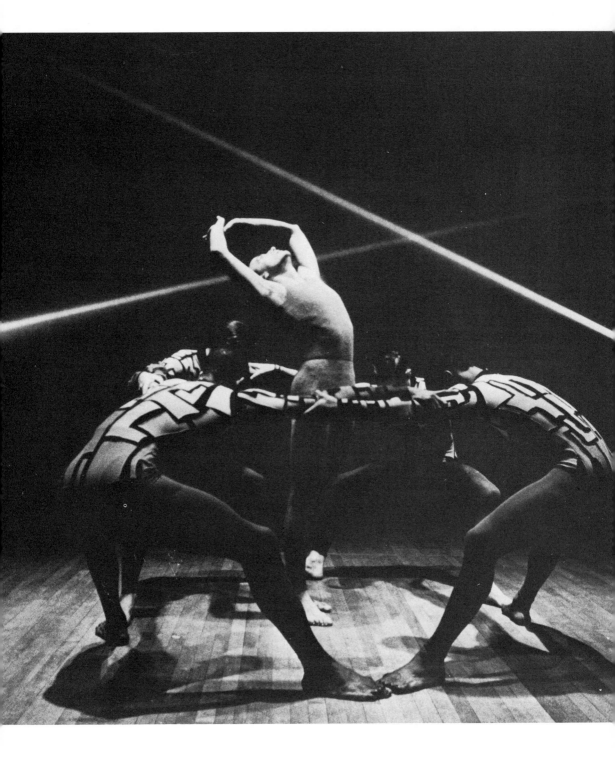

Stages and
Theaters

Stages and theaters mean everything to dancers. They are to a large extent one of the few tangible rewards a dancer can take home with him. To be able to say "When I was at La Scala . . ." or "Did I ever tell you about the time I danced at the Colon?" means a great deal more to the dancer than to anyone listening to him.

To begin with, I envy any dance company that has a permanent home base. Without any doubt the security and familiarity of one's own stage inevitably makes for more relaxed performances. But to tour and to travel, as is essential in my case, does have rewards as well as anxieties.

My home base was at the Henry Street Playhouse. There, for twenty years, together with Nik and my other colleagues, I performed and created a great deal of my repertoire. When we first set up the school and performance schedule, the stage and theater were both badly in need of repair. The stage floor sported a dirty ground cloth over a badly splintered wooden floor. The floor-burns on barefoot dancers were painful and plentiful and decent turning was almost impossible.

In some mysterious way the sum of fifty dollars was raised to cover the floor with masonite. The hazards shifted from burns to slipping and sliding. But it was clean. Floor work no longer gave you the black lung disease, but unfortunately the gallons of water used to clean it also curled the edges of the masonite, and soon it was like dancing on a muffin tin.

The following year the gods smiled mightily. William Bendix, the actor-comedian, won $800 on a TV quiz program and gave it to the Playhouse where he had attended classes as a child.

$800! $800! Before I go on, you must roll that sum about on your tongue. You must inhale that sum into the deepest recesses of your lungs. You must savor it, you must taste it. It was a king's ransom, then. It was Aladdin inside the cave of jewels, and it was ours. $800. And it was to be spent on the Playhouse. Now we had to decide what to do with it, how to best use the money.

We could mend the leaking roof; we could repair the cracked and sealed windows; we could put some padding on the butt-paralyzing wooden seats in the auditorium; we could lay down a new floor. The unanimous decision was a new stage floor, and once that gorgeous stage was installed I can say the great Playhouse years began.

In 1958 both Nik and I went on a vacation to Europe. It was the last vacation either of us would ever have time for again. It lasted four months. This amount of time may seem luxurious, but then we were forced into periods of inactivity because there was no work during the summer.

We rented a car in Europe and took off. In England, where we began our trip, we visited cathedrals and theaters, and I have a note before me which I wrote then.

"Curiously the cathedrals have great theater and no performance, while the theaters have great performance and no sense of theater. Perhaps they should join forces again as they originally did."

I was the navigator and Nik drove. We were on our way to one of mad Ludwig's castles, when a terrible rain storm began. The weather turned cold and the storm promised to last the entire day. The castle was some distance off and the roads grew narrow and winding. Nik stopped the car. It wasn't safe, he said, find another place to visit.

I opened the maps and guide books and settled upon an early nineteenth century Schloss, which had a theater in it. That was obviously the place. Back we went, turned left at the junction and started for someplace called Schwetzingen. The storm became a deluge. Sitting in the unheated car, we pressed our noses to the windshield and inched forward. "What did that sign say?" Nik asked. "I think it said something about a boat." "Are we lost?" he asked. "There is a little river marked on the map, but I'm sure there's a bridge over it," I assured him. We continued for about a hundred meters and he stopped the car.

There, through the rain-swept windshield, was a ferry boat, waiting. A man signaled us forward and we drove aboard. In the rain, he collected his fee and quickly took cover in the boathouse. We sat quietly for the brief trip. There was something eerie about the ride, wrapped as we were in rain and river at the foothills of the Black Forest. The boat docked and we drove off following the signs for Schwetzingen.

As we reached the palace grounds, the rain stopped, but great dark clouds rolled quickly across the sky, letting an occasional sun ray spear down. We parked the car, and in that dry moment we dashed to the first of an endless row of entrances which serrated the low, sprawling palace.

There was no-one anywhere. We walked along the bleached and polished wooden floor, staring at the delicate gilt work, the elegant plaster work. We passed a row of long multi-paned windows until we reached another door, and went through it. A woman sat at a table selling tickets. We bought two, and she motioned us to wait. We sat down on the two austere wooden chairs near her. In a few minutes an elderly gentleman appeared dressed in livery and ushered us into the auditorium.

I had never seen a theater as pretty as that in all my life. It was a little painted toy house, ringed with two tiers of boxes. Ahead of us was an unlit open stage. Our usher disappeared and we sat in the dimly lit house, waiting.

Then as a recording of Mozart's *Don Giovanni* began, a spotlight appeared on stage illuminating an elegant chair, upon which a cloak was carelessly tossed and a sword rested. The condensed overture ended and as the serenade aria began, the backdrop rolled up and the stage grew bright, lit by crystal chandeliers. Three wings of painted flats slid on stage to reveal the second stage, a superb drawing room. The aria ended and another began as the backdrop rolled up to reveal a garden in moonlight with trees and a large fountain bubbling with water. We were now looking through three stages, each gradually diminishing as rendered by eighteenth century perspective. As the music rose to a crescendo, the back of the garden lit up and the rear walls of the theater opened to incorporate the natural landscape designed to continue the theatrical illusion. It was intended, I later learned, to allow a coach and horses to drive into view and for the actors to alight from it and make their entrances.

The music ended, the stages darkened from the rear to the front, and with the last notes, the lights faded out on the chair and cloak.

The house lights came up again and we rose and left. We came out into a dark brooding silence. We ran across the soggy lawn before the rains started again and once in the car, back in the twentieth century, we talked and talked and talked.

What destiny had brought us to this place? A wild storm; an unexpected boat ride across a river; a beautiful and seemingly uninhabited palace; a performance with no people, and all accompanied by Mozart.

What an enchantment. I shall never forget it.

Nik: I suppose if one has his own theater he can afford to make it a magic playbox.

Me: We have our own theater.

Nik: And we're going to work our asses off to make it what it must be. Work is the only way we will ever be able to afford it.

That was a day of destiny. We were brought to remote Schwetzingen in Germany to bear witness to an oracle, and brought back with us to the Playhouse on the Lower East Side of New York City a very ancient purpose: theater.

Today as I sit and watch from an auditorium, storm and battle to mount a work on stage, I always ask myself, "Have I fulfilled that oracle? Is this thing I am presenting the purpose?" And when I am on stage performing, I listen very hard for my answer.

The first important theater I played in with Nik's company, outside of course the Henry Street Playhouse, (which after many years of work and investment became a jewel box of a theater), was the Philadelphia Academy of Music. Fashioned after the nineteenth century European models, it still stands among the great American theaters. My excitement about the auditorium so impressed the stage manager, he gave some of us a tour of the building. It was built, as the Playhouse was, suspended above the foundations. It rested, cradled on pillars, which made it acoustically perfect. But this perfection did not extend to the stage, nor to the stage hands who required two days' notice to move a piano.

The Academy still remains in my memory, bearing with it one of the most excruciating dance moments I can remember. The only redeeming thing about the memory was that it didn't happen to me. We arrived a day early and had the opportunity to attend a performance of a ballet company. A young lady, with fortunately substantial legs, went across the stage in second position plié, en pointe. Facing downstage, she jumped in that position to a steady beat in the music, across sixty feet of stage, en pointe!

By the time she had reached the middle of that vast stage, I was so traumatized by the prospect of the distance she had still to travel to reach her inevitable destination, that to this day I react with empathetic shin splints when I hear that particular piece of music.

My introduction to the variety of stages that exist around the world began with my American tours. These extended onto other continents and eventually became a way of life with me.

Before performances, my company and I warm up on stage. We do a complete one hour warm-up and then run through a portion of a dance full out to get the blood moving to performance pitch. A large part of our warm-up is generally on the floor and on our backs, which gives us a great opportunity to investigate the fly of the stage, and the ceiling of the auditorium.

Once in Vancouver at a charming little auditorium, I found myself staring at the little rotunda-shaped nipple which hung down from the ceiling of the auditorium. Everything was painted cream color to give the impression that the ceiling was of one piece. As I swung and flexed and stared upward, I felt something was wrong about that ceiling. When we got to our feet for pliés, the director of the theater came on stage to greet me. (Yes, they used to do that in those days.) Before he could say a word, I asked him why they had painted over that huge chandelier. He had been appointed director after the ceiling had been painted. He looked up and asked "What chandelier?" "There's a chandelier under all that paint," I said. We chatted further, and he left. After the concert he returned with the news that there was indeed a Tiffany glass structure up there and it looked as if it were still intact. He promised to have the paint removed and the edifice restored for my next visit.

Looking up had other results sometimes. In Madras, India we stared up at monkeys swinging from the bamboo lashed together to make up the grid and rafters, until they disappeared. "Oh my gosh," shouted Carolyn as she ran to her dressing room. She had forgotten to close her door, as we had all been warned to do, and arrived in time to see them departing, rouged, smeared, and chattering. They must have had a wonderful time, judging from the mess they made of her make-up, and they left her a few droppings as a "Thank you."

In the Near and Far East the proximity of animals is a way of life. In the huge outdoor amphitheater in Cartage, Tunisia, the toilets were out behind the dressing tents. "Somewhere near the camels, you can't miss them."

When we arrived in Venice to play the Fenice Theater, no one was prepared for that enchanting house. If I had to pick one theater of all the hundreds I've played in, I would say the Fenice is the most exquisite of them all. It is a cloud of powder blue and gold and also contains the most treacherously raked stage I had danced upon up to that point.

Our opening in Venice was one of the worst nightmares Nik has ever gone through. Our scenery and sets were lost en route. They had been flown to Milan and, as of the night before our opening, there was no word of their whereabouts. The next morning no word. Twelve noon, no word and this our opening night. There was nothing we could do, and our manager insisted we all have lunch instead of waiting in the theater. Needless to say, it was a very quick lunch. Nik, then, went directly to the backstage area and the loading door. The theater, like every other building in Venice, was surrounded by canals. "Come here," he called to me, and when I came to the open door overlooking the water, we watched a fleet of gondolas gliding toward us with the equipment. What a wonderful, crazy moment that was.

Talking about raked stages. The opera house in Brussels is built on a foundation of animal hides. I can't explain why this is so, but I vaguely recall there was a very logical reason. Over the years one corner of the foundation began to sink, and so the stage, which was already very steeply raked, took on an additional list toward downstage right.

Dancing on a raked stage is difficult, but manageable if you can keep your feet on the ground; but a diagonal rake, who ever heard of a diagonal rake? In "Calligraph for Martyrs," which we were performing that evening, there was a section where the four men circled in the air, turning as they did so. While our feet were on the ground we could compensate for the downstage pull; but once in the air, the four of us floated closer and closer to the proscenium arch. By the fourth air turn we were practically in the wings, and using the arch to push ourselves back onto the stage. Of course our concentration was shot, and we talked to each other about that gravitational sensation during the rest of the sequence.

There is really no reason to talk about the eight million ugly high school stages I've danced upon in the United States. Like the bumpkins they are in the world of theater, they wear their curtains, like hick trousers, three inches from the ground.

Theaters like other living things exude vibrations. Some welcome you, some hug you warmly, and some want no part of you. When a theater is built to be a theater it knows its place and its purpose. But those eight million American multi-purpose auditoriums really have no purpose. They are awkward and embarrassed with themselves, and that is what they exude to both performer and audience. Everyone is uncomfortable being there.

This aura a theater emits can be found in the largest and the not-so-largest houses. To stand on the stage of the Colon in Buenos Aires and look out over that incredible auditorium, so perfectly proportioned and detailed, is make-believe come true. It is beyond conception in its immaculate rendering and the illusion created by its accuracy. The proportion of the Colon is overwhelming. In contrast, the ambiance of the theater at Jacobs Pillow is so human, so warm, so woodsy, and in June so freezing.

There are three dressing rooms that remain vividly with me. When I return to them, I feel as if I were returning home. One of them is at the Pillow. Partitioned in rough siding, and crudely constructed, it is viewless unless you open the toilet door, which opens directly onto the woods and the home of three pushy chipmunks waiting for handouts. To protect myself from the usual chill, I'm always swathed in layers of warm-up clothes. But somehow I love that place. I usually arrive hours before I'm due, to walk about, stare at the woods, write, smell the pine and decaying leaves and cleanse my lungs, my mind, and my ambitions.

This same cleansing also occurs in Paris at the Theatre de la Ville, where from my dressing room I can almost reach out of the window, across the Seine, over the flower market and touch the Cathedral of Notre Dame. When at about 6 P.M. as the sun drops, sharply highlighting the innumerable carved edges of the facade, I stand solemnly and watch this *pas de deux* performed by art and nature. The effect always humbles me. I feel as if I must start again with everything I have so preciously achieved.

The Gulbenkian Theater in Lisbon is memorable for entirely different reasons; for creature comfort reasons. The dressing rooms are simply elegant. The plumbing, the furniture, the decor and the marvelous attendants at the theater make one reluctant to return to his hotel after the show, where nothing lives up to these appointments.

I also have a thing about elevators. The Kennedy Center, the New York State Theater, the Berlin Oper Haus and a batch of other tributes to the architects' drawing boards have removed the dressing rooms so far from the stage you have to use a transit token to get from one to the other. To get into a modern elevator before you enter the stage area is all wrong, I feel. Nothing Mechanical should ever convey the heart before it is delivered. One's legs should deliver it to the stage. Probably the best designed theater, in terms of proportion and the relationship created between audience and stage, is the Zellerbach in Berkeley. One needs only lift an eyelid or an arm, and the gesture is in the lap of the audience. There is no need to belt a movement a quarter of a mile out, nor inch around the honeycomb of boxes lining the house. There is complete and direct connection with the audience.

I realize I have not mentioned the fronts of houses, or the lobbies of these theaters, and that is simply because I usually enter from the stage door, in the rear, and leave from there as well. I rarely go out front. That is an alien world to me. I'm never dressed for it. I am awkward with people who come to see and not do, and I find I just don't know what to do with my hands or feet.

Dressing room intercom systems are very important to me. Once the house is open, I must have mine turned up. To hear the audience bring their life to the auditorium quickens my blood and prepares me for performance. Although, I remember one afternoon in the Berlin Oper when I was the spectator. I had left the rehearsal hall to return to my dressing room to get some tapes. I was in my room only a moment when I became conscious of an opera rehearsal coming through the speaker. I found my tapes and was just about to leave when my ear stopped me. A soprano voice began to sing and I was rooted. It was a sublime voice and I sat down on a chair, hands folded on my lap and listened. The singing was rich, ravishing, and immobilizing. Just as the aria ended, Robert came to my room to look for me. What had happened to me? I had been away so long. Was there anything wrong?

How could I explain to anyone what happens to you the first time you hear Gundala Yanovitch sing? I wrote her a fan letter, slipped it under her dressing room door personally and went to hear her sing *Simon Boccanegre* the next evening to see if she was as mortal as she was immortal.

The intercom also brings less profound moments. The most charming I can recall was a voice in Italian at La Scala warning the "Bambini" to get ready for their entrance, as a wave of children ran down the corridor in peasant costumes.

One season when I was televising a performance in Stockholm, the company and I visited the Palace there, and the Royal theater which was incorporated into a part of the Royal compound. How the theater was discovered has a story of its own. Briefly though, a reporter while interviewing the king became intrigued as the king spoke about his childhood and his recollections of the costumes and props he played with in the old storage room. Something about the king's description of his royal toys piqued the writer and he set about to find this fabulous storehouse. What he did discover was the Drotningholm Theater, as perfect a miniature theater as exists today. It was as the king remembered, filled with crates of gowns and robes, armour and arms, props and stored scenery, all original eighteenth century. An historical theatrical treasure was revealed.

When we visited it, we were taken on a special out-of-season tour, and had the place to ourselves. What a happy day.

The auditorium was a long room with rows of wooden benches. I'm sure the audience brought their own pillows and I hope plays were brief, because those were hard benches. But the *pièce de résistance* was the stage, the stage machinery, and the backstage apartments.

The wings were slotted so that the standard sets depicting scenes of various rooms, or of heaven, or of fantastic places, or the outdoors, could be slid on stage quickly. There were two rows of waves that came up from the floor and could be operated by wooden turns and screws to move in such a fashion as to give the appearance of a calm or stormy sea. The thunder machines and firemakers and all the other spine-tingling devices were there. The fly held the heavy wooden machinery for raising and lowering those bound for heaven, and the floors held the elevators for the less virtuous, who were going down. Built behind all of this impressive tribute to those early theatricians was for me a much more sensitive and telling environment. The performers in those days also lived in that theater. Apparently there must have been a resident company. There were several apartments. While everyone else was running about delighting in the stage scenery I remained in the apartments.

The rooms were small but beautifully proportioned. They were well lit and the fireplaces looked as if they could cast a sufficient warmth during those long Scandanavian winters. A few pieces of furniture were placed about the room and from these one could imagine figures seated, dining, and sleeping. There was a wig stand on a table in a corner, which further filled the room for me with boxes of costumes, shoes, hats, make-up, and laundry. Suddenly these empty chambers lit with a blue Nordic light became a jumble of vivid people and clothing and food and rehearsals, and hot and over-crowded and screaming voices, all of which drove me back to the present. I realized, for whatever comfort that realization might bring, that most performers have a similar temperament and the echoes of that vitality remain in every dressing room. When I enter a dressing room, no matter where it is, I ask myself, "Who used this room before me? Did they complain, as I do, about the dirt, the broken mirrors, the bad plumbing? Did they sing as they made-up, as I do? Did their performance go well; were they prepared or anxious?" If one knows how to listen, a dressing room can say a great deal.

Stage floors also have a story to tell. "Treading the boards" is a wonderful old theatrical phrase; it speaks of a noble tradition, a heritage of great performances, mighty artists, a history of an art which has weathered all sorts of political, social, and artistic upheavals. But treading the boards barefoot evokes other feelings. The modern and contemporary dance is usually barefoot dancing, and the protective craft of the boot cobbler is not available to those tender soles. For the past hundred or so years, theaters and opera houses were designed with floors constructed in such a manner as to permit them to be lifted in sections, leaving large spaces between them to circumvent. The floors were later also laced with tracks for scenery and kick stages to be swung on and off from the wings. Every stage floor had trap doors or some facility to open and allow a poor sinner to go directly to Hell, as well as create a properly terrifying entrance for the Devil and whoever else lived down there. In addition the heavy sets of the nineteenth century needed to be securely braced. The fiercest stage screws were sought. Screws that were guaranteed to cut through any wood, and eat their weight in splinters.

Dramatically the floor was usually employed for heroic death scenes. No one lay upon it unless they were down for the count, because floors were noted for their rich accumulations of tradition, called dirt. Any actor who was unfortunate enough to enter drawing a heavy cape behind him, and then having to swing it for an impressive exit, usually left the stage in a cloud of dust and derisive laughter. In the United States the theaters are not as old and consequently have several decades less dirt, but they are doing their best to catch up with their European cousins' tradition.

The past few decades have forced a change in theatrical house-cleaning. As barefoot dancing became more popular, and common practice, the new term "cleaning the stage floor" entered into the theatrical stage management vocabulary. It took a great deal of tutoring to teach the expression and even more patience for stage crews to understand its full and deepest meanings. Clean was never in their vocabularies. Sweep yes, but clean, what was that?

In India, sweeping was a task allocated exclusively to a certain caste. The sweepers would beat the dust off the stage every morning until it rose in a huge cloud overhead. The dust waited patiently up there until the sweepers were through beating and then would descend and settle comfortably from where it had been disturbed. I watched this happen for weeks, but never questioned its inscrutable wisdom.

In the last decade the light, transportable Marley floor has become a solution to the clean floor problem. Prior to that, ballet companies carried their own stage floors or coverings. These ranged from ground cloths, a heavy canvas pulled tightly at the edges to minimize wrinkles and accidents, to staggeringly heavy linoleums. Aside from a good hardwood floor, those old linoleum floors were wonderful. Today progress has relegated linoleum to the obsolete ward, where it has become an endangered species. Linoleum is no longer produced in the U.S., except in rare instances.

In Europe and the U.S. most theaters have floors for dancers and some even have floors reserved exclusively for barefoot dancers. Ballet floors are usually saturated with resin, and when the sweat from bare feet mixes with it, an unpleasant compound results, called glue.

In spite of all these difficulties, things on stage have improved enormously. (I, however, have solved these endless hassles, coward that I am, by carrying my own floor with me.) I have spent a great deal of my life on stages, for all of their goodnesses and faults. Although I am a citizen of the United States, born and raised in New York City, and a traveler to every part of the world, when I am asked at passport control, "Where is your home?" I am always tempted to answer, "Onstage. Why? Is there anywhere else?"

New York City

Identity:
The Me-Factor

Throughout my career I've been interviewed a great many times. They have been held primarily by newspapers and television interviewers. Quickies. Instant depth. With reporters I would chat for an hour or two at the very most, and with television appearances it would usually be "live" and I'd be questioned anywhere from three minutes to half an hour. In that limited time we would talk about life, art, finance, New York, Nureyev, modern dance as it differs from ballet, audiences, the growth of America's art consciousness, touring, what dancers eat, and then cap it off with some professional advice for talented four-year-olds. Then we would give equal time to the concert I was currently plugging. Time, place, where, how to get there, and where to get tickets plus a short description of the show.

When one has gone through this many times, the answers become as commonplace as the questions. There is really no excuse for this other than the pressure of air time. The only excuse I can make for myself is that I honestly don't know where to begin.

"Tell us about yourself."

"What do you want to know?"

"Tell us about you. What is a dancer really like? What brought you to dance? What do you get from it? Do you enjoy it? Why are dancers different from, say, myself—ordinary people who also like to dance and admire dancers very much?"

"Whoa, hold up. That's a lot of questions. Let's start again."

"All right. Tell us about yourself."

Then I proceed to give an historical account of birth, school, study, and achievements. We usually discuss the past. If there is any extra time, we talk about "What exciting things the future holds in store," which, when put that way, again invites the commonplace.

I usually get a chance to talk about everything except the Me. Who is Me? How does one talk about the Me? Where does one begin? What is the make up of the artist? Who is the person onstage, and who is that other one offstage? Who is the one that creates, and who is the one that worries about shopping and laundry? Why is it so difficult for an artist to talk about himself without contradictions either in word or deed? Granted, with maturity his views will change: from the trusting student always yielding to guidance and safe on that trusting plateau, to the young artist tempering everything with a prescription of inexperience, curiosity and fear, to seeing finally with eyes that have grown worldly with familiarization and careless with habit.

It's more than that; it's the complexity of an artist's make up. It's *many* Me's that make up *the* Me.

I've lived with artists all my life. Some good, some great. I've attended performances of, or looked at, or read, or listened to artists of the past, also some good, some great. I've wondered, as have others, why Rembrandt seemed so determined to ruin his life, and I've marveled that Schubert managed to survive his brief one. What raged within Beethoven, Modigliani, and Raphael when all the while they were producing perfection?

I've known artists who spoke like morons while practicing their genius and others whose fatuous natures never prepared anyone for their depth and power. I've heard some artists interpret their own work and miss the boat entirely. "Surely," I thought, "this isn't the same man talking who made this piece?" And I was right. It wasn't the same man. Same body, but occupied by a very different person.

Artists have always been the misfits of their society; they've never been part of the mainstream because somehow it's difficult to get a handle on them, to know who you are dealing with.

When the same man appears in a suit to talk business with a board of directors or at a senate hearing, and then changes into a wild outfit for a kookie opening night, or flashes his ass in a performance, and then arrives the next day to teach a children's class, it becomes very difficult to know who you're dealing with.

Why have artists always been written off as unstable? What is that strange perverseness that will bring them to the winning line only to refuse to cross it? Why do they always seem to change their minds? Well, it isn't a matter of changing their minds; it's a matter of which of the multiple persons in that body is foremost at that time.

Artists know they are comprised of different personalities. As a matter of fact, most people know this. Everyone has somewhere along the line experienced that split. But artists develop not one, but several personalities, and not whispery, shadowy figments, but clear-cut defined people, some more outspoken than others.

There is first the Person-Me. The name on the social security card and the thumb print in Washington. For myself, there is also the Performer-Me, the Choreographer-Me, the Teacher-Me, the Writer-Me, the Cinema-Me, and the Artist-Me. It takes a lot of skill and physical strength on the part of the Person-Me to keep the reins on this thundering team. Artists go mad for a number of reasons. The first is that they fail to understand that these other Me's must be allowed to grow and identify themselves. To thwart them is to tear oneself apart. Secondly, once these others begin to assert themselves, they must never be put in the driver's seat alone. The Person-Me must always be nearby. Some of these other Me's operate on a purely spiritual level and have no understanding of the physical limits of the body, whereas other more physical Me's sometimes don't know when to stop whipping themselves. The flagellant and the effete sit at the same table, but with different appetites.

It isn't enough that a performer recognize that the role he is playing on the stage can influence his own way of living. He must accept the fact that there are definite and separate people living in his body, and that they each must grow with their own values and that often these values contradict each other. Outsiders can get very confused by these contradictions unless they are made to understand whose voice they are listening to at that moment.

I've developed a great many inner voices and an equal number of inner ears. I've had many a five-person conversation within myself. I have no idea what the Choreographer-Me looks like, yet I've had endless talks with him. I've heard him scream with exasperation and frustration, and I've helped him beam his success and satisfaction.

I've seen photos and films of the Performer-Me which have, to varying degrees, impressed, piqued, or on some occasions made the Person-Me uncomfortable. As for the Teacher-Me, once I caught a glimpse of him in a studio mirror. It was fleeting, momentary, before he realized he was observed and returned my look. He seemed distressed. His eyes seemed very deep. And yet, the photo released of him teaching shows him radiant, elated with his observations.

The Person-Me is a loner, with great patience, and low-keyed. He pulls to the back of crowded rooms. He gravitates to bookcases and actually looks at paintings on the walls. Fine craftsmanship intrigues him, and he'll investigate wood moldings and furniture details and trace the intricacies of oriental rugs. He can spend hours and hours sometimes during the hottest part of the day in his hopeless garden weeding between weeds. He will stare endlessly at the relationship of different plants in juxtaposition to different light, squinting and opening his eyes to see them still differently. Once, and he confessed this story only to Nikolais, he stood so still, a chickadee alighted on his head and proceeded to shell a large sunflower seed. The Person-Me was at first terrified at the bird so close to his eyes, but he remained immobile until the bird pecked the seed open, ate the nut, and flew away. After which the Person-Me roared with delight and jumped and jumped to think a wild bird had trusted him so.

But what is most characteristic of the Person-Me is his inertia. Give him a book, and he will lie down anywhere and finish it. He has a large library and has read about seven-eighths of it. The *Encyclopaedia Brittanica* is dipped into at least once a week, but he no longer retains the minutiae of our civilization as he did before. Of late the Performer-Me has begun to claim all of the available memory banks to hang onto twenty-five years of dance counts. I also have a faint suspicion that a good deal of his reading is done out of habit now and not, necessarily, from the pleasure of the written word. Now he reads to fall asleep.

He is mellowing, though, there is no question about that. He has developed an aversion to the contemporary art of the 1950s and 1960s. He'll walk out of the room if certain advanced music is being played, and he doesn't use the word "interesting" anymore. Recently, I noticed his language is being laced more with obscenities than usual, but that could be a throwback to his old navy days. I hope that is all that surfaces from that salty era. I don't think my heart could stand up to his other earlier appetites.

The Person-Me does the resting and eating and organizes the logistics of who is to occupy the body. The Person-Me is amiable about food. If the Performer-Me must eat certain things, he goes along with it, and if the Creative-Me demands endless coffee, he goes along with that, too. The one limit the Person-Me insists upon is limiting quantity. He will not overeat, and for this the Performer-Me is most grateful. Alcohol frightens all the Me's and the

Person-Me will drink his vodka when no one else is inhabiting the body, which is usually late at night after a performance.

Teacher-Me is in a class of his own. Generous to a fault, his compassion for and involvement with the art never ceases to amaze me. He is quite selfless. He gives and gives and often gives what doesn't belong to him. Choreographer-Me and Performer-Me have often slapped him down for revealing insights they don't care to share with anyone else.

Teacher-Me has also the kind of patience that a good teacher should have. Performer-Me has none. Once in the midst of watching student compositions, Performer-Me began to rise from the chair.

"Where are you going?"

"You don't expect me to watch anymore of this, do you?"

"Are you crazy? Sit down."

"Get me some coffee."

He must have seen someone nearby drinking from a thermos. Other than that I have no idea why he asked for coffee. I have never had any particular liking for coffee before. I got him some and ever since then that is how I sedate him. I now drink a great deal of coffee with lots of cream in it. I think coffee is being included in my contract.

Teacher-Me is obsessive about a great many things. How students are managing their lives, what they eat, where they live, do they hold their chests up out of class, why are there rings under their eyes. Who needs encouragement, are they improving, what jobs will be available to them when they are ready. Forcing the creative outlet. Building a compositional skill. Forcing a strong technical base. Understanding release, totality, transition, dynamics, quality. Verbalizing criticism so that it is objective and not personal. Presenting the principles of the art and directing them towards the future and not the past. Using the past as a point to measure how far we've come. The work, the discipline, the persistence, the breakthroughs, where are we? and who are you? Performer-Me, however, will look him straight in the eye and callously say "Who needs it?"

Teacher-Me is not sentimental, but he abounds in compassion. He is concerned with everyone, a preposterous goal. Since he deals with so many students, he carries very little over from the day before. Each day must, of necessity, constitute a new horizon. For the teacher there is only growth. And growth is today and tomorrow, not yesterday. Yesterdays can clutter the mind and the vision.

On concert tours Teacher-Me usually takes a back seat. But on the Indian tour as I lay writhing with dysentery on a hotel bed in Bombay, I half-welcomed death and half-feared it, because they would have to stretch me flat out to put me in a coffin and lying doubled over was the least excruciating position I could find. As I lay in a semi-delirium half singing, half moaning, Teacher-Me, very cool, very authoritatively took over. He firmly told me to stretch certain muscles, round my upper back, lift my legs. To roll over, put my feet to the floor, and then waited, as a spasm swept through me, before he continued to guide me through my recovery. As far as he was concerned, I was just another kid gaining strength and learning to walk.

Have I mentioned his sense of humor? How he leaves the class with a lightness? He believes strongly that the vibes in class must be light. Spirit is so fragile. So much can be broken with a heavy hand. Besides, these are going to be the happiest days for a long time. The classroom is where you can and should make mistakes. "Come on, dolls, what have you got to lose? Let's see that open chest and that open face, and get rid of the 'vacancy' sign hanging from your nose. I know someone is in there, and better still, you know it too, so let it out."

Later on, away from classes, it's not so easy to keep it light. Things get a little heavy. No one is around. Not many seem to care. It's important to learn how to pick yourself up.

Teacher-Me is the moralist, and like all moralists, often drives a good thing into the ground. His vocabulary includes words such as honor, truth, beauty, honesty, and other anachronisms—hardly someone you'd take bar-hopping or allow to be interviewed on Kalamazoo television. He's also, curiously, the fighter. At nine he took on the bully of the block who was intimidating the smaller kids, of which he was one. For this excursion into justice, he received a broken nose, but also stopped the bully. His objective devotion to his profession has also developed a watchdog instinct in him. While he's around, no one is going to bully this art. That's strong talk and the other Me's are conscience-racked as to how to handle this possibly career-destructive tendency.

The Choreographer-Me is the easiest to live with. I suppose it is because his working habits are part time. He's constantly observing figures, forms, relationships, light, and anything that moves. Occasionally he'll try a movement phrase at some inappropriate time or place and embarrass the hell out of the Person-Me. The Choreographer-Me is the brain of the family. He can conceive floor patterns for large groups, develop rhythmic structures, translate his intent into the principles of his craft, and, in general, range out over the abstraction and mechanics of movement. He is also the most childlike, probably because he stays apart and lives in his own world so much. He delights in everything. Seeing a form take shape, being able to make successful corrections, losing faith in a piece when it doesn't work at the first run-through, embarrassed with success, crushed with failure, like a child he responds to them all as if for the first time.

There is one bad period when he makes himself distinctly unwelcome in the mutual house. This occurs during the early germinal stage of a new dance. He has a disturbing and sometimes painful habit of throwing all the nerve endings to the outside of the body. While he is in this tactile receptive stage, everyone else becomes touchy and irritated. During this time the Person-Me starts a new book, the Performer-Me works on leg extensions, but the Teacher-Me doesn't turn his back; he tries to help.

He tries to organize the sparks that are flying and igniting everything around. It's not an easy time, but fortunately it doesn't last too long, only until the next time.

Things have changed for him, as well. Working with companies other than his own has put him under additional strains, and here too, the Teacher-Me has come to his rescue a thousand times. To dancers unfamiliar with his vocabulary and movement qualities, the Teacher-Me has turned many a rehearsal into a mini-class. It is at these rehearsals that the Performer-Me has a bad time. He loses his patience constantly, as usual, when other dancers cannot perform a phrase as well as he can. Once in Berlin, a visiting choreographer attending one of my rehearsals, watched me demonstrate a solo for one of their lead dancers. Afterward he said to me, "You know, you didn't show him how to dance that. You showed him how he will never dance it." Since then I've restrained the Performer-Me considerably from demonstrating. I'm also working on restraining him from making derogatory remarks when he watches other dancers perform movements he can dance better. At least he doesn't say them aloud.

Of all the Me's, the Performer-Me is the most vivid. When he moved into the body he took a fifty-year-lease and started renovating immediately. Nothing suited him. The legs had to be changed. The hips relocated. The chest lifted. The neck stretched and for ten killing years he reshaped everything. Nothing evaded him. Nothing was secret. He savaged the heart, the mind, and the tear ducts. He charted a single course to create an eloquent instrument of movement and nothing was strong enough or developed enough inside to challenge him. He was an autocrat, a tyrant. The body had to speak the language of dance, and he would not tolerate any impediment.

There were nothing but classes, rehearsals, and performances for ten years, until the endless physical pain found solace only in numbed exhaustion, and then more classes, rehearsals, performances. The entire placement of the body was shifted. Muscles were always strained, nerve endings always pinched, glands always swollen, feet torn and split. But, by God, when he was through he made a dancer to be reckoned with.

Volatile, mercurial, strong, and a temper from flaming to passionate. There was nothing retiring about this personality, and every curtain was the starting line of the Preakness Stakes.

The Person-Me had absolutely no control of him and did everything he demanded. The Person-Me ate, rested, and behaved only as the dancer demanded. And please let nothing go wrong in performance because it only meant more rehearsals and always the pain.

But the ecstasy of a perfect performance was also too much to bear, and it was in one of those raptures that the Person-Me awoke in panic and never let the Performer-Me play the tyrant again.

It was during a performance of "Journal" in the slow dance before the finale, when everything came together. The movement, the energy, the flesh, and the spirit, and as I began a slow relevé, the Performer-Me said, "I'm going to levitate." The Person-Me was terrified and pulled back. "No, no. You'll disappear, you'll go into a fourth dimension—don't!" "I'm going to."

"Don't," and with that the two Me's locked horns. I finished the dance but after the concert the scene in the dressing room was an ugly one. I realized that without some boundaries the Performer-Me could be self-destructive, and in this instance, mad.

I realized that he was alone too much. There was no one in there to share the body with him. When he was alone, the stillness was shattering. He needed someone to talk to, and so the Person-Me and the Performer-Me became friends. Fortunately, they both have a great sense of humor, and often I've rocked with laughter listening to them. There's peace in this body because those two get along so well. I'm lucky and I know it. I've seen other artists pulled apart by incompatibility and with no possibilities of divorce. The Performer-Me has very little regard for some of the other Me's in this body, and I've seen him goad some of them mercilessly. There's no question that the Person-Me must always be present when the Teacher-Me takes over, otherwise the Performer-Me begins to ridicule and bully him. Fortunately, the Performer-

Me is a night person and I usually teach during the day. It's the patience necessary for teaching that drives the Performer-Me up the wall. He cannot bear listening to the reiteration that is so integral to teaching, and keeping him still as he watches improvisations or compositions is like taking nose count in an ant hill.

The Performer-Me keeps his relentless legs to the grindstone. The show is always the thing. After performance, when the Person-Me is belting down vodka, the Performer-Me keeps out of drafts, complains about the air-conditioning, cuts the fat away from the steak, keeps his eye on the clock, and calls a limit to any latenight disco dancing.

With Choreographer-Me his attitude is entirely different. On rare occasions he is almost respectful. But whatever the scene may be, he is always a "pro." Having an in-house choreographer calls for another kind of collaborative discipline, and Performer-Me knows that. Whatever Choreo-Me sets, Performer-Me does. Performer-Me knows that Choreo-Me has extended his movement vocabulary enormously. Dancing barefoot on some of the worst stages in the world has made me very adept at bandaging my feet. Turning on splits and opening them further is like something out of the Spanish Inquisition. Choreo-Me has evolved a series of heel turns that Performer-Me has mastered very discreetly without throwing his weight back. Performer-Me dances whatever Choreo-Me sets, full out, then writes it, then rehearses it until the neuromuscular memory knows it cold, and then shows it to Choreo-Me. But it is in performance that Choreo-Me often makes his changes. Something happens to the Performer-Me on stage that he can't bring to early rehearsals. He's told Choreo-Me that only in performance can he reconstitute the choreography. That's when the juices flow.

In performance the Performer-Me dances for one certain person. He places that person in the audience every time and rises to that person's expectations. For him, Nik is always out there, and praise from him is enough. But, oh boy, what a height to rise to before you get that praise. Once about twelve years ago, exhausted and surly, I gave a really lousy performance. He saw it, and still refers to it. Imagine, after twelve years. But he has let up a bit. He concedes now that everyone is entitled to one bad performance.

Performer-Me loves cats. Person-Me is allergic to cats. I lived with a cat for eighteen years. Guess who calls the shots in this body. Menasha, the cat, was skittish of Performer-Me because he moved too fast, too unexpectedly, but adored Person-Me because he was always lying flat on his back and reading quietly. She'd (why I named her Menasha is another story) curl up between his legs or on his belly and sleep. I took allergy shots, tried not to touch her, kept her away from my face as much as possible while Performer-Me grabbed her, kissed her, played violently with her until she raked his arms, causing the Person-Me to go into an enervating attack of sneezes.

Teacher-Me also admired cats. Schmutz, at the space on Thirty-sixth Street, was a great favorite of his. She sauntered into composition class once, when he was trying to verbalize a particular awareness necessary in dealing with time. Schmutz demonstrated it so clearly that the class applauded, which scared the pants off her, and she tore out of the room.

To further confuse matters, two other Me's are beginning to demand equal time. The Cinema-Me and the Writer-Me, both of whom have very specific orientations.

How oblivious the Me's can be of each other was made clear to me these last few months. I've been going through absolute hell with the renovation of an old house. Workmen, contractors, architects, finances, decisions—pure hell —when suddenly, in the midst of all this the Choreo-Me set up a rehearsal schedule and slowly and methodically began choreographing one of the best dances he's done in years, and finished it. One part of me would go to bed frustrated and in tears every night, while another part of me would lie down so pleased and so proud paying no attention to the utter dejection in bed with him. Incredible.

As I put the razor to my throat every morning, commonly called shaving, we all get together, and everyone complains. I don't know how Person-Me stands it. He probably doesn't hear it anymore. With the patience of a wonderful mother of a large family going quietly about the job of getting everyone off for the day, Person-Me goes through a morning ritual that includes something for everyone. Checking out the gray hair, the bags under the eyes, the stiff ankles, the vitamins, the weight-scale, the fresh rehearsal clothes, chocolate bars, the drum sticks, a writing pad, a book, the thermos.

It's strange that I can talk so freely about all these Me's because lastly or perhaps primarily there is the enigmatic me I've never seen, the Artist-Me. I can hear him walk the deep corridors within. He lives in that shadowed part, lit only by the single purpose.

When I reach too deeply, I can feel him. I can feel his presence. I can feel him reaching out, and I close my eyes and let him enter me. I dare not look. I am afire, I flame, he passes through. I hear him round the bend. I can breathe again. I am flesh again. I open my eyes to see where he has been, to see what he has touched.

What if some day I should innocently open the wrong door and stand face to face with him? Would I be consumed? Would I be terrified of whom I might see? Is this why I close my eyes and open my senses when he appears? When he possesses me, whose eyes do I use? I know it is his handiwork when I cannot explain what I have done. Does this vague visage know me any better than I know him? Who would recognize their own soul if they should meet it?

"Tell me," asks the interviewer, "Tell me about you. The Artist-You."

"The Artist-Me? I don't know him. I've never met him. I know him only when I dance, only when I create, only when I'm alive."

I am frankly afraid to know him. He knows the answer, the final answer. I'd never risk knowing that. I'd rather always be reaching than arrive.

Washington, D. C.

On Teachers

Dancers aren't really a forgetful lot. They can memorize twenty or more roles and keep them at the tips of their fingers or toes. They rarely forget curtain time or rehearsals. They remember the phone number of their chiropractor and, under the worst pressure, still remember to take their vitamins. Choreographers are also fairly responsible about remembering things. Their recall is considerable, often down to remembering to order flowers for opening night. It's a gift they share. Yet, I've often wondered how easily they overlook, or frequently forget, an intrinsic part of their careers: their teachers, where it all began, who taught them to walk.

Perhaps in one's search for personal identity it is only natural to shed the cocoon of the classroom. Perhaps the standard of the formative years is the level all growing things measure themselves against. In pushing forward, one forgets to look back. Unfortunately, when the classroom is forgotten, the teacher is often put aside as well.

Teachers are the unsung heroes of the profession. Audiences don't know who they are. Dancers, through familiarity, take them for granted, and many choreographers often wish they would produce better dancers.

The classroom and the teacher are the closest thing to stability a dancer knows. In the environment a teacher creates, the dancer learns trust. The studio and the teacher, no matter where they are, are the kitchen, the hearth, and home. The air is permeated with sweat, warmth, and belief. Everything is answered, in silence or in words, by the teacher. No one will hurt you in the classroom unless it is best for you to be hurt, or you hurt yourself.

The voice, a touch, a word. Comfort, challenge, answers, faith, direction. A teacher makes eyes shine and sweat glisten. A teacher can say to the greatest dancer "You were good today!" and the dancer knows greatness again. A good teacher can tell you not only how, but why, not only where you are, but who you are.

Who are these people who teach? These people who so desperately care for their profession, for their students, for their art? Where do they come from? Where are they found? Why do they teach?

There must be a designed order that spots great teachers throughout the world in strategic places and another order that leads the potential artist to those places. In the triumvirate of dancer, teacher, and choreographer, I've always felt the teacher an equally important member, because everything that takes place on stage begins in the classroom.

What makes a good teacher as opposed to a bad one? Well, basically a good teacher feeds the class, and a bad one feeds from it. What they feed, and how they feed the class constitute their uniqueness. If the students absorb, then the teacher has taught. The absorption can range from an intellectual flickering to an artistic mastery of the body. How wonderful it would be to say that all teachers are good teachers, that virtue is always rewarded, that justice triumphs. But unfortunately teachers don't create the fairy tales, although they are often forced to live them.

No other profession than the arts is marked by greater extremes. The business responsibilities on one end are almost alien to the artistry at the other. Yet the teacher must be able to reach out with both hands and join together the economics and ethics of the art.

The range of teaching goes from the daily classes of a great dance company to the after-school basement-studio, toe, tap, and baton lessons. The schools that are associated with companies are underwritten by those companies. The schools that are sponsored by patrons can be counted on two fingers. For the most part, teachers must handle their studios and schools as profit-making businesses. Classes must accommodate extreme ranges of age, and some of the courses offered serve no other reason than to "make a buck."

The business world has very few ethics. Only the law restrains them from outright dishonesty. What sort of environment is this for a teacher dealing with artistry?

What a life!

And yet, there are great teachers, beautiful people who give and nurture. If they question these economics, they keep those questions out of their teaching, because of their inherent dignity, devotion, and dedication.

I take the maxim, "There are only two kinds of dancing, good dancing and bad dancing," one step further—"You can't have good dancing without good dancers," and good dancers do not pop out of Cracker Jack boxes. They are born and raised and somewhere along the line good teachers have gotten their hands on them.

Some teachers use their classes to exercise their own egos. Some use the class to impart sterile patterns. Some don't give a damn about teaching; they are simply forced to do it. Some are terrified of it. Others are inspired, articulate, and knowledgeable people who shoulder the responsibility of recognizing talent and bringing it to fruition. And yet they all teach.

Where do teachers come from? The first answer to pop into everyone's mind is Shaw's old chestnut: "Those who can, do; those who can't, teach." But one will also notice that the chestnut has remained a hapless chestnut and has never grown into a mighty oak of truth.

A good teacher, out of simple reason, has to have in some way participated in his art and, through this participation, come to teaching. It is also true that many performers consider teaching or coaching after their performing career has ended. Their contribution is invaluable and essential. Professional experience can only enhance professional teaching.

Performers and choreographers have a great deal to impart to students and the next generation. This impartment is, after all, the only direct link we have to our heritage. There would be no dance profession if it depended to any degree upon the printed word. The nature of dance is such that only in the doing does the art speak. Only through dancing does the art exist. After I had been viewing the scene for many years, it became obvious that, since teaching prepared the dancer to perform choreography, it was essential for teachers not to drop out of the performing "scene" but to keep in active contact with rehearsals, choreography, and performance.

Teaching "steps" is as bad as choreographing "steps" and performing "steps," and the aridity of "steps" occurs when the three get out of contact with each other. Together they constitute the fullness of the art.

Students are what teaching is all about. Facing a parade of sizes, shapes, temperaments, egos, surliness, radiance, and a cluster of unhappy, gorgeous, malformed, vibrant, obstinate, trusting, dumb, and talented kids is simply facing a daily class. Students usually bare two major characteristics of the young —selfishness and trust. They are selfish in their demands and trusting in that they know you'll meet their demands. Students can also get very attached. They are a little like cats—never doubting their bowl will always be filled, but resentful if you go away for a weekend and leave a stranger to fill it.

If you ask dancers when they started to dance, they will talk about when the spirit overtook them. But ask teachers when they heard the calling, and they will grin wryly. Teachers aren't often called; they are usually pushed into the profession.

My teaching career began at the Henry Street Playhouse when *they* decided that the afternoon hours were to be filled with children's classes. When *they* decided that the income was necessary. When *they* decided that the long tradition of children's classes should be continued. When *they* decided that I should teach them. I was led into a room filled with children, the door was closed behind me, and my teaching career began.

The next fifteen years were years of love. I took hundreds of kids through their childhood and adolescence. Professionalism, or a career in dance, never entered my vocabulary. They were brought to dance as a living experience, yet they worked with a stronger dedication than many adult professionals I have taught. Dance meant something to them. It wasn't just steps. Of course they believed in me, they trusted me, and that belief was one of the greatest responsibilities I have ever faced in my career. Although I have since stopped teaching children, I always remember with great affection my years with them.

I would arrive, Saturday morning for a 9 A.M. class, sore and exhausted after a Friday night performance. There they were, expectantly awaiting me with days of accumulated exuberance. I fed them and they supped. After five hours they left and, drained and exhausted, I could turn my thoughts ahead to the evening's performance.

I remember one day in class when things had gotten out of hand. My patience was stretched, my nerves taut. I had lost control of the energy I had stimulated. I stood in the center of the room and grimly waited to grab the first kid who passed me and show that class that I meant business. My reasoning had sunk to that level. When I felt someone behind me, I turned. A little seven-year-old figure, waist high, came closer and leaned against me. I hovered over my victim. Then she looked up and said, "I'm standing close to you," and I melted. It was then that I understood that the profession had its rewards. The child was not being sentimental, but in the midst of my chaos she had made a simple statement of order. Teaching became for me a way of practicing order, or, as Nik says, sanity.

The rewards of a career in the arts aren't exactly going to win first place at Dun & Bradstreet nor rate a bronze bust, but fulfillment of some sort is expected. In this profession, the dancer has the direct satisfaction of the doing, the choreographer has the satisfaction of realizing his choreography, but the teacher must wait to see the results of his giving. Sometimes he must wait years for this reward. Sometimes it seems a lifetime.

Dancers and choreographers pace their careers with short-term investments, with performances and opening nights. Teachers have longer commitments and tend to see the forest, not the bouquets. Commitment is a very difficult idea to define.

I teach because I want to know more about my art. I suppose in a way I'm a scientist. I question and I answer. I dissect principles to get at their pulsing hearts. I drive my classes until I've split the molecular structure of a given movement phrase. I experiment, I distill, I clarify, and I keep out of the way of my discoveries. Dance has its own identity, and I teach it objectively. But being objective is not easy. Teaching can be a very subjective business.

Dealing with students is a constant tempest. How do teachers ever get reconciled to the inevitable exodus of their best students? Even admitting that that's the name of the game, it is still heart-rending each time a favorite or a talent leaves. What can a teacher say when a third-year student, after taking one class elsewhere, breathlessly announces a major breakthrough? How does a teacher face a kid who has worked diligently and hard and tell him he just might not make it? How much does a teacher interfere with a talent who is ruining his life with a screwed-up head? When does a teacher cry "halt!" to a student who glibly takes what he has been taught and teaches it as his own elsewhere?

Experience prepares teachers to teach. It is only through teaching that one learns to teach. It is only through teaching that one knows what he knows and learns how to present and articulate it.

Preparing for the profession doesn't necessarily begin with a teacher-training course. I had a professor during my college years whose offensiveness was so thorough it could only be protected by his tenure. He turned off just about everyone taking his classes. I realized then that if I ever taught I sure as hell knew what I wouldn't do, and that was to turn kids off.

What draws teachers to this profession, aside from earning a livelihood, is the inherent understanding of the important role they play in keeping the art together, and the accepted realization that they have been chosen to play that role.

Everyone in the profession goes through the classroom. The classroom allows everyone the chance to achieve his own identity. Hopes, dreams, and ambitions are all played out there. Physical release, which is the core of the dancer's need, is practiced there. Only dance—the nonverbal language of the art—is spoken there. There is no need for apologies, just achievement. And at the helm of it all is the teacher.

The teacher stands at the crossroad of the dancer's world. One rein on the creative, one rein on the technical, one rein on the aesthetics, one rein on the living process, one rein on the future, one on the past, all of them straining at the same time. With the skill of a Roman charioteer he maneuvers this thundering energy towards some goal. The Muses pause to watch. Another flight has been made; another class has been taught.

New York City

On Curtain Time

Performances do not begin with the house lights dimming and the curtain going up. They can start as much as hours before curtain time—or never, if the viewer is unreceptive.

On a Friday in January, I went to see Claudia Gitelman dance at New York University's Loeb Center. It seemed that everyone I met or spoke to insisted that I see that last of her three concerts. Hanya Holm had choreographed a new solo for her, and the word was out that a rare and beautiful thing was happening at the Loeb.

By 7:00 PM I finally got out of the rehearsal studio and by 7:30 PM I was out of the building. I estimated the walk to Washington Square to take fifteen minutes. It took twenty, and once there I didn't know where to go. The lobby was filled with students reading, studying, bustling, and I could see no immediate evidence of people oriented toward a concert event. I walked toward an armed guard for information, but he was focusing on some obstreperous kids in a corner, and that discouraged me, so I investigated on my own. Along the back of the very large lobby-lounge, I saw a line of people, and walked toward them. I saw first one, then another familiar face and concluded, "This must be the place." It was almost concert time, and I suddenly realized that I did not have a ticket, and with this enormous line waiting to get in, I could very well miss the performance. Fortunately, someone from the ticket desk approached, took me by the hand, and passed me through.

I found a seat, took off my coat, muffler, hat, gloves, boots, and collapsed. I was exhausted. It was the first chance I had to catch my breath all day, and my energies sagged to the bottom of my wooden chair. (What a way for a concert to begin! What an unfair handicap I was placing on the artists! They were now faced with lifting me from my own distractions into their world. I was bringing nothing. I was too tired. It took two dances before I could bring my sensibilities to an evaluating level.) The environment was a large room with bleachers and chairs on the viewing end and a nicely proportioned performing space at the opposite side. My eye quickly hung decent curtain legs over the inadequate ones which existed, and my imagination supplied everything else necessary to make a performing environment of the space.

And then there it was, that breath-suspending aura when an artist enters the stage: gorgeous, golden Claudia appeared. Bare, beautiful feet. A lifted, vaulted abdomen that echoed a breathlessness. The lower spine, lengthened and powerful. The head and eyes, clear and transporting. Arms which, when they curved and reached, sung of a depth of expression. The rapport between choreographer and performer was obviously one between two mature artists. It was a memorable performance and anyone who missed it missed something special.

And then compare this pre-performance with another, a concert in London. An hour before the concert my energies and excitement were high. I had the time to select not only the clothing I was going to wear, but my jewelry as well. I boarded a large, clean London cab and arrived at Covent Garden where I was admitted backstage. Nureyev was warming up onstage, and I chatted a moment with him, and was then led into that ravishing theater. From a perfect seat, I watched a high spirited performance of "La Fille mal Gardée." In London the concert began an hour before the performance and in New York, as late as two dances into the program.

Concerts also begin or never get off the ground depending on the audience's frame of mind. I remember sitting behind an annoying man and woman at a performance by the Royal Danish Ballet at the Met. The woman exuded an aura of the most uptight resistance to what was occurring on the stage. Her companion fed from her hostile reactions and never once allowed himself his own opinion. He cued from her discontent. I was appalled, and I had no choice but to react since her intense bitterness radiated about ten feet. She cast a pall over the evening. Compare this with audience atmosphere at a Joffrey concert. Here the auditorium is always warm and gemütlich with positive vibes, and no matter what is performed, the audience takes it to its bosom.

For me, the most intrinsic factor of curtain time is when the curtain goes up in the viewer's mind. Six people sitting together in the same row watching the same concert will see six different shows. The veil that can blanket the eye or color the viewing is the veil of receptivity. How much easier it would be if the artist did not have to spend time tearing a hole through the veil, if the viewer could simply lift it and allow viewing.

But who knows the numerous influences which impair or hamper viewing. To a goodly extent each viewer sets his own stage. For some people the curtain will drop with a thundering crash at the first sound of electronic music. A hint of garlic to a fastidious nose and wacko sensibilities withdraw. A persistent cough or a noisy candy wrapper from the next seat and you might as well call a cab. Even the comfort of the seat is a consideration. An insulting or surly usher can keep the curtain down all night, while a long slow revenge is plotted.

Once at a ballet performance at the State Theater a fist fight broke out three rows in front of me. Imagine, at a ballet program, two guys slugging it out! One of them had been dragged there by his wife and he began muttering disparaging remarks which the other fellow found insulting to the performers. The people around them pulled them apart and separated their seating arrangement. It was no wonder that when the stage curtain rose, the curtain on my perceptions was still down, and as for those two men, you could rest assured it was going to stay down for the rest of the evening.

There are so many possibilities for distraction which can dip the curtain: the voices of children uttering infantile wisdoms, usherettes wearing jangling bracelets (one of Nik's pet peeves) and doing target practice with what feels like a ten thousand watt flashlight when it hits the eye. And if you should be caught in the rain before the show, you can feel the starch seeping out of everything. People who plow up the aisle with determined haste to leave the theater at what you thought was the best part of the evening can also cue the curtain's descent.

As long as I can remember, there has been a running discussion as to whether one should eat dinner before or after the theater. Some say it dulls the senses; others feel they can concentrate better when they are not listening to their stomachs, and as for getting loaded before a show, I agree that a warm cozy seat in a darkened theater is the best way to sleep it off.

Sustaining interest is also a problem. I don't mean the interest of the actual performance, but interest from the time of ticket purchase to the day of the show. As so often happens in New York for a hit show, the ticket must be obtained so long in advance that sometimes one has to be reminded one has tickets for the theater that evening.

With so many possible distractions threatening to prevent an audience from giving its fullest attention to a performance, perhaps someone should make available a preparatory course for playing the role of spectator. The New School should offer a course in Audience Preparedness. This course, A.P.1, should not be confused with Theater Appreciation (T.A.1) or even offer any experiences in attending the theater, but be designed more along the U.S. Marines Obstacle-Course Manual. It would be a survivor's guide to viewing. How to keep the curtain up once the lights go down. It should include what and where to eat before a performance. (If you can afford it.) Who to take with you. (If you're afraid of the dark.) What to wear. (If you've never sat for three hours in a small seat in tight pants.) Self defense. (If you take sides.) Concentration. (If you haven't read the program before the lights went out.) A necklace of garlic. (Especially if the standing room is crowded and you're in the center.)

But putting all of this aside, more important than the curtain rising is, when does the curtain fall? How long does a vision, a memory, an impression remain? I remember so vividly attending my first theatrical performance on my ninth birthday—a performance of *Pinocchio,* presented by the W.P.A. Theater Project. When the curtain went up on the second act, the blue interior of the whale glowed before me. At that moment, like Guipetto, I was also swallowed up, not by the whale, but by the theater. And to this day that curtain has never come down.

New York City

On Nureyev

first met Rudolf in London. He came, together with Glen Tetley, to my dressing room. I was in the process of taking a bandage from my foot, and he stood quietly by and stared at my efforts until I finally removed it. That was the moment that endeared him to me initially, because in those few minutes we talked silently, we talked foot talk. I don't think anyone but dancers understands the reverence we have for our feet. "How do you do that?" he asked. I promised to show him how I made the special bandage I used when my feet split.

I met him again, backstage in New York, and later again at a large dinner party in a foreign embassy. It was during this time that we talked about working together and "Moments" was decided upon. That was in 1975. Since then I've gotten to know him well, and we've become close friends, I think.

Immersed as I've been all my life in the modern dance scene, totally caught up in its evolution, its travails, its comparatively unglamorous work patterns, and contrasting movement vocabulary, the ballet world always represented some alien planet orbiting "somewhere out there." I'd seen some extraordinary ballets and watched some marvelous ballet dancers, but other than as a viewer, my involvement with that world was nonexistent. Then suddenly I was totally involved with the Berlin Opera, The Royal Danish Ballet, the Scottish Ballet, and Nureyev. For whatever reasons this came about, it changed my life by sharpening all my attitudes toward the dance profession as a whole.

Rudolf and his intensity brought a new focus to my already intense outlook. This I think is one of his important contributions to the dance, this intensity and how it has affected everyone who has worked with him. After working with him one is forced to re-evaluate one's convictions and the capacity of one's output. There is not a class, a rehearsal, a company, a performance that he has attended where he has not left his mark, the mark of his own fierce intent. His silent and sometimes not so silent challenge has been, "Are you working as fully as you could?" "Again!!" he says as he lifts his settling body from a chair, and "again" it is. "Once more—no?" "Let's get on with it."

Up until this time modern dancers had for the most part initiated the association with the ballet vocabulary; Graham, Cunningham, Taylor, Ailey and others were doing a great deal of bare-footed ballet work in their dances, as well as training their dancers in the ballet medium. What had begun in the 1930s as a revolution against the ballet technique looked, by the late 1970s, as if it would end in quiet capitulation. It became a common practice for dancers and choreographers trained in the modern dance idioms to transfer their interests to include ballet.

Then suddenly Nureyev came over from the other side, again! For however personal his reasons may have been to expand his movement experience, Nureyev must get a great deal of credit for building the bridge from ballet to modern dance. Although others had attempted it, he took the plunge, he took the largest gamble, he had the most to lose. He saw this other movement vocabulary as something he had to try, and above all he had the courage to do it, not as an experiment with one choreographer, but as a steady development with several. He saw it too as an investment in his future. It was inconceivable for him to retire from dancing at the height of his physical prowess and he had no intention of doing so. The modern dance promised longevity to his performing career.

He began awkwardly because he learned his roles as steps, as most ballets are learned. Gradually he realized that a different vocabulary and a different resulting communication was possible, and he set about grasping all this as well. Challenge is a large part of his diet, and by his own admission, he has only begun.

Rudolf takes class wherever he is—in opera houses and in studios of every nature. Most of the other dancers in those classes do not perform much, and for them the class offers them their only opportunity to dance, which they use fully. They do their ninety-nine fouettes, their twenty pirouettes, endless beats, and in general knock themselves out; whereas the performers in the class know that the 11 A.M. class serves basically to wake up and warm up, not to exhaust themselves, because there are still hours of afternoon rehearsals to face before the evening performance. When a luminary enters the studio, the "kids" see this as an opportunity to test their mettle. I'm so amused to see their disappointment when nothing happens. To see their expectations gradually drain from them while the visiting artist goes about the business at hand slowly, methodically, and dispassionately. As Rudolf stands at the barre or waits his turn to come across the floor, draped in layers of tattered warm-up clothes, he is pacing himself for another twelve-hour day of dance. To compete is the furthest thing from his mind. He won that race a long time ago.

His daily regimen has only one purpose; to prepare for, and to dance. He rests, he rises, tea, class, tea (In rehearsal his body pours out perspiration freely, and he pours tea with plenty of sugar just as freely back into himself. "Rudolf, do you want any tea?" "Always" he answers), then lunch, unless someone forgets to bring it, and hopefully it is black bread, smoked salmon, rare beef, thick butter, and sugar, then back to rehearsal, hours of rehearsal, and a massage scheduled in somewhere along the day. If his masseur, Luigi, is not with him, then he faces the anxiety of finding someone who can massage "long muscles" as Luigi does. The nap usually lasts two hours, then three hours of performance, dinner, and on into the night.

He has an almost blue-white skin, which he claims comes from eating so many potatoes as a child in war-starved Russia, and a scar above his lip where a dog bit him. He is still cautious with dogs. Only at home with Claire, his housekeeper, and at the tables of cooks he knows will he eat anything other than rare meat. He cannot afford to upset his physical mechanism in any way. He is wary and frightened of drafts and keeps his head covered when he feels one. A knit cap or a towel will suddenly appear on his head in the studio or in a restaurant if he feels a breeze. After food, he lets down a bit and his mind turns to sex. He is in a way a glorious combination of a lot of good training and a lot of hard living. His living is not geared to life, but rather to dance, which is the only life he knows.

In rehearsals Rudolf is not always in his best form or on his best behavior. Who is? Rehearsals are hell. They hurt. Doing a new movement over and over again gets to new muscles, and muscles get to nerve endings, and nerve endings have long pointed teeth. Endless changes can also exhaust the memory process until you can't remember anything and if one is tired, memory failures are easy. Memory failures are frustrating and tempers grow short. Rudolf is a formidable person and a powerful presence. When he flares up and curses, he is impressive; and even if he doesn't flare up, his curses are still impressive. They are earthy, picturesque, amusing, unintelligible, obscene, and almost always effective.

The "short temper" of a performer should not be considered seriously or taken out of context. Tempers are an important part of the performer's survival kit. The temper potential equates somehow with the performing potential. Exercising one's temper is part of warming up. Tempers are warmed up with irritants. I've seen or rather heard Rudolf warm up his temper, with something as simple as the condition of his shoes, their color, their fit, and their elastics, to the wrong ballet decor shipped from abroad with an opening night two days off.

Since dancers work so physically close to each other, whether they wish to or not, they often become part of the friction factor. But usually when tempers cool, one can hardly remember what they were raised about.

One must also understand a little about partnering. Relating to another person on stage demands a great deal of effort and cooperation, both of which come from the energy reserve of the dancer. To support a partner properly, one must understand and know his partner's role. The man must supply a great deal of strength to allow the lady to dance properly, which she can only do if her balance is secure. She must be able to trust him and rely upon him so that she is free to employ gravity and momentum. She also depends upon his sensing her preparations for lifts. This calls for a sublimation of the man's ego which is very difficult to expect. Giving up one's ego on stage is indeed a great deal to ask of any one, especially performers. Nevertheless they do it. Their relationship at the least must be *sympatico,* at best a union of love. This often carries over from the barre to the bedroom.

In the classical ballets, partnering was the primary function of the male dancer, but in the past twenty years they have found themselves more and more in the driver's seat with prominent dancing roles, and are less willing to step down and pull the wagon again.

I make no attempt to excuse reluctant partnering behavior. I only try to explain it from the inside, to explain what an effort it is for the male dancer to go from direct projection to standing behind the lady and trying to project through her, from prominence to structural support.

Pulled and strained muscles are very common to men during partnered rehearsals. A bad preparation can throw a back, a shift of weight can pull a muscle. It is understandable that men are reluctant to jeopardize themselves, and it is easy to see why tempers grow short.

Rudolf must dance with ten or fifteen different partners a year. If he works amicably with five, that's asking a great deal; the others can tell you tales that would chill your blood.

Rudolf curses like a trooper; "fucking" modifies every noun within firing range. He's unaware of his language because like a trooper he no longer hears it. He works like a trouper and curses like a trooper. You can imagine the flutters this creates in "Tutuland." Next to massage, nothing is more soothing to tired feet and pinched nerves than loud, healthy cursing.

It's not that Rudolf's temper is any worse than other artists'; it's just that he is so towering a figure that everything he says seems to carry more weight. Once, alone in a dressing room, he let loose with a stream of curses, about what I can't remember now. "Fucker-mother," he said and since there was no one around, I corrected him grammatically. That took him off guard and he was very amused.

He drives himself mercilessly. I have seen him hover on the edge of exhaustion so many times, dancing with leg injuries that would hospitalize anyone else. He has a dread of hospitals and would sooner trust "old wives' medicine" than penicillin. Surely those around him must excuse the condition of his nerve endings that motivates his temper. Frayed muscles, frayed nerves, frayed tempers—everyone who cares about him begs him to rest. But he won't because he fears that stopping to rest will mean stopping forever. This is not his nightmare exclusively; all dancers past thirty-five fear this, especially men.

He is not the ogre he is often made out to be. He expects everyone in ballet to work at his level, and when they fail to rise to it, he bites.

One should also talk about his sense of humor, and one should also talk about how wonderful it is to see him laugh. He does some excruciatingly funny imitations; he's witty and some of his puns are pretty good. He mugs all the time. This lighter side is not generally known, unfortunately.

One night after a performance in New York we were having dinner together with a small party. The table was set in a semi-enclosure which made it difficult to seat more than ten people. While drinks were being served two more guests joined us. We all decided it would be easier to squeeze a bit rather than change tables. As the first course was being served, Makarova and her husband appeared. To accommodate them we all squeezed closer still. I was wedged between Rudolf and Makarova.

I asked her about the new baby and her health. Both were fine, she answered. She carried with her now a small notebook, she confessed, because when she was pregnant she had a great deal of time to think, and now she had to know answers. She was writing things down. This helped her. Then almost immediately she and Rudolf fell into deep conversation. Like two conspirators they conversed intensely in Russian. Both were pressed so tightly against me, I could have been another body attached to theirs. Rudolf had her hand in his and both their hands were resting on my stomach. I managed to free one of my hands and continued to eat, maneuvering the food to my mouth without interrupting them. I felt like a mother with two children on her lap.

Being far-sighted, their heads were too close to my eyes for me to see them clearly. What I could discern however, was their bone structure. On one side was Tartar Russia. High cheek bones, fierce eyes, and intensity. On the other side was the Russia of the Icons. Oval face, almond eyes, tilted head, nodding compliantly as the Tartar spoke. I am sure if Baryshnikov were there, his hand would have also joined theirs and the three would have found their communion back to Kirov and back to the heart and soul of Russia, which none of them have ever left or ever will or can. No matter how long they live in the West, they will always be Russian. No matter how they insult and slander each other, they are a family and can never be separated.

When their conversation became too animated and I found eating too difficult, I asked them what they were discussing so heatedly. They stopped, a little sheepishly, pulled aside, and Rudolf with a smile said, "Would you believe it? Fouettes." I roared laughing. But in a moment they were at it again. "Tell me about musicality," she asked Rudolf. He explained the difference between the way they know musicality at the Kirov and in America. He told her among other things how Broadway theatrical dancing routines restructured rhythmic phrasing, and how this influenced Balanchine when he first arrived in America. Then they spoke again in Russian. "Russian is a difficult language for answers," she said. "The words have so much emotion and so many meanings. It is not definite like English."

"It is because Russian is made up from so many dialects." Rudolf added.

I could not but think with a little anguish what it must have been like for him when he left Russia. A frightened kid, on his own, taking a gigantic step. The press must have hounded him mercilessly in every language other than in the one language he could speak effectively and understand—Russian. From that moment, he could trust no one. Dancing was all he knew, and all he could do. Where in the West was he going to do that? In the early days he received far more advice than opportunities. Although he could dance, he had to learn to stand on his feet as well. Only on stage was he safe. He could understand that language fully. Off stage he was always apprehensive of the English language, of the press, of the people, of his family, of the future. Although much has changed, the stage is still the one place he trusts. His one stability, his only home. That is one of the reasons he performs so much.

One will rarely see him "dance" in rehearsals. He "marks" a great deal. Only in performance does he dance full out. This is maddening to his choreographers, who cannot tell what they have created unless they see it. This is why they watch him so intently during rehearsals, and why he doesn't often work twice with the same choreographer. Somewhere in the run-throughs, he'll flash out and give a clue as to how he'll perform the movement. He'll rehearse a piece over and over and over again until his body knows it. But first he must know it in his mind. There is, however, one clue to his rehearsal pattern. He has three or four rehearsal garments which he always wears, one over the other. When he has them on at the same time, looking like a rag picker, it means "forget it." He is rehearsing now for himself. Gradually he begins to peel them off, and gradually one begins to see the dance. The closest one will see him rehearse to performance level is when he is wearing only one unitard. Sometimes he will make the transition from his memory to his muscles and the heat of performance will overtake him. The extra clothing will just roll off. Two pairs of tights will drop to his thighs, making it almost impossible for him to raise his legs, and the extra leotard straps will fall off his shoulders almost pinning his arms to his body, but he'll be oblivious to this straight-jacket and continue on to the end of the dance. You cannot imagine the fascination this creates for anyone watching him. One expects to see him land on his ass any minute.

When I work with Rudolf, it is important for me in the early rehearsals to see him dance everything at performance level, once. After that I don't bug him. If I've seen it, I know he can rise to it again in performance, if he cares to. Because I hate rehearsing myself, I let him get away with murder. The two of us have to push each other to rehearse.

I, myself, rehearse in pieces and parts and not always in the studio; sometimes alone, at night, in the hallways, while eating, on street corners, in the shower. Rehearsal for me means one full-out performed run-through. I hate cleaning up, I hate going back, I hate going over and over pieces. I have no patience for rehearsals. They make my head ache, and also "pros" shouldn't rehearse like "kids." Kids learn confidence, stamina, performance techniques, continuity, and other things during rehearsals. Pros conserve their energy. Like I say, one good one a day is enough. I know this is terrible advice for young dancers, but what the hell.

Rudolf's memory and his memory processes are impressive. One can almost see him brand the choreography into his mind, and when one also considers the complexity and similarity of ballet steps compounded by the innumerable versions of the same ballet he has performed, that prodigious memory of his becomes still more impressive.

I treat movement as an abstract vocabulary. The passion of fulfilling the movement is its drama. The recounting of the energy within a phrase is its story line. "What does this movement mean?" he asks me. I answer "On the 1 count, let me see the shape, 2–3–4 you draw the peripheral in space with your arms, on 5 and 6 you release the weight and drop. On 7 and 8 you rise creating a diagonal parallel between your arms and left leg. That's what it means." He says "Okay."

He is everywhere performing different roles. For anyone else, his schedule would be madness, and indeed anyone else would go mad. But for Rudolf these are the only bounds which can contain the restlessness his energy creates. He cannot walk, he must hurl himself. His schedule just prior to one New York season reads: five weeks Paris—"Romeo and Juliet" (Nureyev version); Amsterdam—rehearsal and performance, and learn two new pieces; Toer van Schayk's "Faun" and vanDanzig's "Dark House" and the opening solo from "Canarsie Venus" and "Vivace" with Louis; to Copenhagen to video Taylor's "Aurelio;" to London to film a program for Margot Fonteyn's BBC series; to Milan to stage and perform in "Sleeping Beauty;" to New York with the Louis Company and Dutch National, then lengthy tours and a season in Paris where he and I will appear on a program together for the first time. All the while, his schedule is being blocked in for two years in advance.

There is little middle ground with him when it comes to money. I cannot remember seeing him wear jewelry, although I'm sure he has some, and he is always without a watch. This is perfectly understandable—two-thirds of his waking hours are spent in taking off and putting on his clothes. It is easy to lose or forget things in a studio at the end of a long day. One is usually so tired and foggy that the homing instinct is often the only thing that gets you to the dressing room to change.

He is either frugal or extravagant. This is so clearly indicated in how he dresses. Since he spends so much of his working day in the studio, his rehearsal clothing is important to him, yet it is almost always in tatters. Almost everything he wears in class has holes in it. This is generally the case with most dancers; the runs and tears in their rehearsal clothes are like the cuts on a tom cat's nose, evidence of challenge and dubious victory. One would think it an affectation to see Rudolf dress humbly, until he sees the black mink coat thrown carelessly in the corner, or draped over his sweating body en route to the canteen.

He expects others to pick up the restaurant bill when he is their guest, and as a member of the profession, he expects to be passed through at any performance he attends.

Rudolf is box office. He can fill any house anywhere, anytime, and anyplace. He knows his value on the commercial scene and he is astute about it.

Since his name speaks box office, it doesn't surprise anyone how many hungry mouths appear in the nest, waiting to be fed when he performs. Expenses rise astronomically. Everyone wants a piece of his action.

When *The New York Times* wrote of "Millionaire" artists, they were a little misleading about his getting $10,000 for a single performance. I'm sure he can command, and does on occasion get a figure as high as that; but why didn't they also mention that during his many, many years at Covent Garden with the Royal Ballet he drew only a fraction of that each week.

Charisma is an interesting word. It's usually associated with the mystique of performing stars. Yet I know stars who have it and others who don't. For some it comes naturally, while others have to work at it. Personally I feel that those who can claim it do so because it happens in spite of themselves. Although charisma appears in many guises, it has to do with how that star burns energy.

Some flame, some spark, some smolder. Some are intense while others burn evenly. The energy can be restless, erratic and on occasion, destructive; but no matter what form it takes, it is almost always unpredictable. The viewer is never quite sure when something is going to happen or where or what. It is this expectancy that lures the public. The thing they have been waiting for can happen at any moment, and they could not live with themselves to know "it" happened and they were not there to see. Charisma is disruptive. It draws its public insidiously. It tantalizes, it makes promises, it is a voluptuary willing to bathe the public in the sensuous delights of expectancy. "Will this be the night?"

There is no question that Rudolf has charisma. His public never knows what he will do or say, and all the while cares desperately that he will do it or say it when they are there to share it. Rudolf's charisma is marvelous and disturbing to be near. Everyone wants something from him. Many aren't even sure what it is they want. It's enough to be near him, to watch. He is life. He is removed. He is never attainable; one must always reach. They tell him little things of the life they feel they shared with him. "Rudolf, I did this," "Rudolf, I saw you here," "Rudolf, I will see you again soon at such a place." "Rudolf," (unspoken) "we will always be together." They are both male and female. They are of all ages. They are reverent, they are patient. There is something holy that occurs when he stands among them. He says little to them. Their communion is generally in silence.

Once waiting in the wings watching the phenomenon of his curtain calls, someone nearby asked me, "Does he really believe this?" "Yes," I said, "if he doesn't believe in his bows, he believes in the reason for them." His reason is his public. Audiences cannot be lumped together under one general category.

They have distinction and purpose. Audiences have needs. They are not simply ticket buyers. Some feed, some take, some give, some follow, some lead; but whatever roles they play, they most always lend purpose to the performer. Rudolf's audiences, his following that is, come to live. They come to live through Rudolf's life and to a great extent Rudolf's life on stage exists to keep them alive.

It is a symbiotic existence. At the end of a performance, through his many bows, he brings them down gently from the ecstasy of their union. It can be no other way. It would be callous and ruthless to end the affair hastily and to drop the curtain. Keeping the curtain raised keeps both of them alive that much longer, breathes life in both of them that much longer. They both make the moment last as long as possible.

It would seem needless to talk about Rudolf's artistry. Surely his reputation is based upon solid achievement. He is a superstar of virtuosity and passion but equally important is his curiosity, appetite, and courage about and with everything surrounding him.

He reads every newspaper he finds. He attends music concerts, dance concerts, films, plays, anything performed by people or animals, sometimes two or three events in one day. It doesn't matter what the hour, he's ready to go. He exhausts everyone. He must know, he must see, he must hear everything. He is passionately fond of music. He carries a cassette library with him, and now more than ever, he immerses himself in music. Only don't ask him to sing, because he will, and eventually hopes to on stage.

He must have opinions about politics, after all, he is an intelligent and well-read man; but he will not utter one word about the subject. He did not leave Russia because of politics, and he is still a Russian citizen, at least as far as he is concerned. He left Russia to dance a broader range of roles, and there is no dancer in the profession today who has danced so wide a spectrum of movement. When this epoch becomes history, it will be recorded that he helped shape the dance profession while others were shaped by it, largely by his overwhelming drive and single vision.

He has not yet committed himself to the modern dance, and I don't know if he can or will. His training, his life, his bones, and his heart are still totally devoted to the classical ballet. How can one divorce from oneself?

I remember at La Scala he was teaching a young man a sequence. The dancer repeated the phrase, but it didn't work. Rudolf rose from his chair and walked onto the rehearsal area, and danced the steps. I cannot tell you how beautiful it was. Everyone in that room was awed, because out of nowhere he performed glitteringly. "Rudolf," I said, "you were truly fabulous." "You see" he answered, "I don't think I can ever leave the ballet. These legs are ballet legs, I would have to take them off and put on modern legs. But not now—later. I feel too I must pass on to others what I know, what I have, what I am."

Rudolf is alone a great deal, although he is always surrounded by people. But being alone is a great deal different from being lonely. The first is by one's own choice, the latter is by the choice of others. Rudolf is not lonely. But he is alone often during his travels regardless of his exhausting social calendar, and it is so important that his hosts know this and look after him. His presence is so awesome, it is easy to assume he is without human needs. But regardless of his superhuman output, he remains quite vulnerable, especially to the passage of time.

There is a heartless syndrome in the classical ballet. It could literally be called role playing. There are two roles for men to perform. The young dashing boy burning with innocence, and triple *tour en l'air,* never growing beyond the age of courtship, or the old man obviously past the age of pirouettes. There are few, if any, roles for men. It's either boys or crones; cavaliers, or characters. One goes from dimples to putty noses. It is indeed a depressing prospect for men, to have a life time skill judged only by leaps and turns in the air. What of the physical excitement of strength, balance, extension, stretch, intensity, projection, maturity, and the richness of gesture. When will we hear "The Princes are dead, Long live the king?"

Rudolf fled Russia to dance. Perhaps, unless the ballet creates substantial roles for mature men, he might have to flee the ballet to continue dancing. Shortly after Rudolf's fortieth birthday, Walter Terry wrote of me in *The Trib,* "Fifty year old Murray Louis is unquestionably the greatest virtuoso that modern dance has ever produced . . . he displays a mastery of the body that is incredible."

When people ask me, "How long can Rudolf continue dancing?" what can I say? "Ten, fifteen years? Who knows? Anyway, Happy Birthday, Rudolf." And remember, when you're the best, take it from me, you can only get better. *NA STROVNYA*

Paris, France

On Revivals

One of the difficulties in discussing revivals is that everyone has to admit his age. Worse still, there are no inbetweens when you talk about revivals. You are either young or old; young if it was before your time; old if you saw it. Everything about revivals seems to focus on time.

Is the piece old enough to revive? Is the time right? Is there a new audience? Will old-timers care to see it again? Will it show its age and suffer from the consequences? Does it have appeal for today's audience?

There is also something festive about the opening of a revival—the young in the audience hoping for some insight from the past and the elders hoping that this moment will bring their present into focus. Little do they both realize that only a percentage of the past will take place, and part of that will be in their own minds.

One day in 1950 Nikolais came into the studio at the Henry Street Playhouse and said that Ruth St. Denis had just called and said she would like to film one of her dances on the stage, and in turn would do a concert for our children's series. He sounded very doubtful as he told me this. "You agreed, didn't you?" I asked.

"Oh yes," he replied.

"What's the problem? Why do you look that way?"

"She needs ten men to dance in it."

We looked at each other and burst out laughing. Is that all? Ten men? I know this gets lost in the translation, but twenty-five years ago to find ten men in a dance studio was like trying to reassemble the original service for twelve from The Last Supper.

Finally, by using the brother of one of the dancers, the two orthopedic cases, and the kid from the children's division who was tall for his age, we assembled the ten men. An assistant to Miss Ruth appeared and began rehearsing us. He assured us immediately that there was nothing to worry about. The choreography was simple and there was enough time for rehearsal before Miss Ruth joined us. We told him how we managed to assemble the ten dancers and he admired and encouraged us. After the first rehearsal, he assured us he couldn't tell the orthopedic cases from the others . . . which, after my first sigh of relief, I didn't think was very funny.

The choreography did prove to be simple. There were basic floor patterns which were designed around Miss Ruth, and if the counts were too difficult, we could phrase with the music. The piece was called "Gregorian Chant" and used chants for accompaniment. We walked and swayed in lines and circles and formations. The fervor we brought to those rehearsals was unimaginable. Terror, I'm sure, accounted for much of it. There was one form in which we made a large circle, sank to our knees and did a very slow backbend, all of us trying to touch our heads to the floor. The circle we could do. The lowering to our knees didn't go so well—there were always a few sudden crashes to the floor —but the backbend was the killer! It was pure agony, and if we once took to laughing at our inability it was over, down to the floor we'd go.

We asked the assistant what Miss Ruth's path would be during the dance. "Oh don't worry about that. If she gets near you, just get out of her way."

And then she arrived.

Well, what can I say? To begin with, she was eleven feet tall, iridescent, and was surrounded by a five-foot magnetic force. She greeted us and the rehearsal began. Some of us froze now that the moment of truth had arrived, but we went on. She watched us as we danced, and when she approached anyone, the line would buckle. We reached the big climax, and down we all went to our knees. We were beautiful, not even a knee crack. Into the backbend —it was all clear sailing after this—but as I arched back, head touching the floor, I heard a voice saying "Not so far, young man, not so far." As everyone else swept up and over I flattened out and went down. Once the determination went out of me, I couldn't maintain the form.

We finished the rehearsal and shot a good performance later that day. The film did capture the fervor we brought to it—made up of fear, determination, and an engaging lack of skill.

The key, I would say, to reviving a dance like that today would be, not to assemble a company of well-trained dancers, but to use a group of half-trained dancers who would make up the other half of their limited skill with determination. The structure of the Denishawn dances was extremely simple. Its complexity rested in the performers. St. Denis and Shawn were not simple people. Books have been written about what motivated them.

The recent revivals of Denishawn make it apparent that there are two factors which must be considered in revivals: the kind of dancers needed to dance the less complicated choreography of the time and the quality of the soloist.

The most evident thing about Miss Ruth was her aura. She literally glowed. When I saw her she was in her sixties. Off-stage she walked with such weight and difficulty you didn't think she'd make it to the door. But on stage she was radiant, and through some power, so transcended her physical being that the word "magic" constantly came to my mind. She had the sort of flat foot that Indian dancers have from dancing on stone floors. She was big-boned and everything hung loosely. Half her life was spent with the gods, and the other half seemed to have been spent touring.

Shawn was much more physically oriented. The energy of his dancing and the muscularity of his male dancers gave him his distinction. He was more conscious and deliberate about performance. When I got to know him, he had long ceased to dance, but he was never offstage. I did see him dance, however; I saw the two of them together. They were stars.

Not only do dancers today look differently and dance differently, they think differently. One would have to cast very carefully for a revival. An overly trained dancer does not have the skill to bring richness to simplicity. When they are called upon to perform the squareness that generally characterized the structure of revived choreography, they don't know what to do with all their technique and consequently overact the role to release their untapped energy. To extend and hold your leg in a high second position and then whip it into a double turn was pretty hot stuff for a modern dancer at one time, but today, what with all those yoga classes and wheat germ they're taking, they can wrap their leg around their head and turn four or five times and then ask you, "What's the next step?"

Dancers with this skill can only smile and hope everyone understands how they are humbling their virtuosity to bring you the original thrills your grandparents fancied.

The body proportions are also different today; the modern dancer has suffered particularly. The ballet influence has ironed a great many lines of character from his body. It is difficult to find a scruffy ball of fire today. It seems to be all placement and pliés. The pugnacious thrust of a heel could set the space around the modern dancer to boil. But this has been noticeably refined by the cooling effect of a pointed toe. Some years ago at Connecticut College, Graham's "Primitive Mysteries" was revived. I sat between Bessie Schoenberg, who had danced it in an early Graham company, and Nikolais, who remembered seeing a very early performance of it. They had both come with enormous appetites and had left so unfulfilled. Throughout the performance they both commented on what had been changed, what had been left out, what had been gussied-up. I had to insist they both be quiet so I could see the dance. When the curtain fell, they both went at it again. Bessie had been in it and saw it with her backbone. Nik had been outside of it and saw it with his eyes. I began to think then about whether revivals should be recreated from behind the scenes, behind the footlights, or from the front of the house.

They both agreed that the dancers couldn't dance the work as it needed to be danced. I knew some of the dancers who performed the work and realized again that it wasn't any technical inability. They were overtrained and could not restrain themselves enough to dance simply, although the choreography for its time was very rich.

Audiences are also not the same. The early modern dance audience was small, select, and often derisive. It took them a while to respond to abstraction. It was easier for them to respond to the dancers' efforts.

Béjart, who for many years had been ignored and kept out of Paris, was finally invited to do a work for the Paris Opera. Of all things, they asked him to restage "Giselle"—or something like that. He took the job. "What can I do?" he moaned to me. "These girls arrive to work in tight pants, boots—chic, coiffed, on motorcycles and I am expected to awaken in them the romantic past of a hundred years ago. Impossible!" (You have to say the last word with a French accent. It says a lot more.)

I know that I'm particularly sensitive to the use of fabric on stage, having worked so carefully with it for so many years. When I saw the scarves being used in a recent revival program, my first reaction was: "They've gotten the wrong material for those scarves—the wrong weight and texture." I know it sounds picky, but when you're using fabric to accompany you, you've got to get the right partner.

John Martin tells of Fokine, who was brought in for the final touches of a revival of Nijinsky's "Les Noces" in Boston. The girls were in a line, making tracing gestures from their heads to their waists. Fokine gasped, turned and chokingly cried, "The braids! Where are the braids?" (Try saying that in Russian. It really comes through.) The gesture had been revived, but not the reason for it.

Cyma Rubin, who produced the revival of "No, No, Nanette," wrote into the contract of the dancers and singers that they could not wear wigs for the production, and that their hair was to be bobbed—or no job. "The fashion of that period was based on the natural bobbed look," she insisted, "and if I have anything to say about it, that's the way it's going to be." Cyma had a great deal to say about it, and that's the way it was.

There are two kinds of revivals: historical ones, and dances which have been dropped from repertory and then are brought back. The historical revival faces a good chance of appearing naïve and ludicrous if it has not aged sufficiently and developed a patina of the past.

It's a hell of an art, dance is. As a temporal art it constantly loses its heritage to time. Imagine having to recreate Mozart with rock musicians or the ancient Greek dances with a modern ballet company.

Historical revivals are very important now for modern dance. Ballet keeps its tradition through revivals. Some ballet revivals are uninterrupted for a hundred years or more. The modern dance seems to have reached a point where its past has come into perspective. The cinema was extraordinarily remiss in not capturing that past; and video, which has been much more responsible about this, has appeared too recently to record posterity.

Time heals, time mellows, and time obscures. Bittersweet becomes sweet. Initials, brutally carved in the trunk of young trees, become touchingly sentimental with the years. Nostalgia, sentiment, and the safety of distance can be disastrous for revivals. It seems to me that to revive a work properly, one cannot bring the work out of the past to create it, but instead one has to go into the past to re-create it.

But then again, now that modern dance is beginning to concern itself with historical revivals, perhaps it should consider what ballet has concluded; since the training of the dancer has changed over the years and audiences have grown more sophisticated, perhaps it would be wise to update revivals, rather than recreate. Almost every ballet "classic" has been overhauled a dozen times, and will continue to be so in the coming generations. How possible either of these alternatives are, I have no idea. But should Hanya Holm revive "Trend," which will be forty years old next year, with the Louis and Nikolais companies plus twenty other dancers, I'll know a great deal more about revivals; whether one should re-create a modern work with attention to historical accuracy, or whether it's better to update, revise, and overhaul in the process of revival.

St. Louis, Missouri

Creativity and Choreography

Words, for all of their specification, are not as accurate as one would hope. Part of the ambiguity lies not in words, but in their usage. People tend to have personal connotations with regard to words, personal definitions. If there is difficulty verbalizing the factual or scientific, then one can only imagine the chaos resulting from attempts to communicate the nonverbal, such as the language of dance.

The practice of art is so intensely subjective, so personal, so seemingly private, it is inevitable that eventually everyone gets caught and trapped in their own sticky web of definitions; still one must persist.

On the level of artistry all arts share a common verbalization. The beautifully evasive "Art speaks for itself," can keep you out of a lot of trouble, but in the lower strata where teaching, the acquisition of skills, and the development of specific perceptions occur, communication is faulty and tends to break down, unfortunately at a time and place where it counts most. There are complete classes taught wherein teachers and students operate within different frames of reference, unbeknownst to each other. In class, teachers are "poetic" and resort primarily to demonstration to illustrate their point. It's safe, it's direct, and if the teacher cannot demonstrate a movement, there is usually someone in class who can.

This pedagogic device is all well and good for technique classes and steps, but is useless in conveying such loaded concepts as creativity, choreography, improvisation, and performance.

As I think back, I can remember when the distinction between creativity and choreography was first dimly implanted in my mind.

We had for years at the Henry Street Playhouse presented student recitals which evolved from the composition classes. These were the result of assignments given throughout the semester. The student's challenge was to create materials relevant to a premise. The premises were simple and were to be explored as directly and inventively as possible. There were always fresh and engaging studies in every class, and the best were selected for the showing. The audience included friends, guests, and the student body.

After three or four of these recitals, the enthusiasm and success they generated prompted us to open the house to the general public.

The first subtle signs of imbalance occurred when the audience became general. It wasn't at all unreasonable; as a matter of fact, it seemed perfectly natural that a few adjustments should be made. The new audience was not as familiar with the classroom orientation as was the student audience and would view the studies with less experienced eyes.

A few lights were added. Rehearsal clothing was replaced by tidy leotards and tights, and a bit of make-up was applied, all of which tended to make the choreography more prominent. The problem then became that the choreography went from prominence to dominance and the whole focus of creativity was lost. The studies looked weak and suddenly made little sense.

"What went wrong?" I asked myself. "These kids are creative. The studies were original in the studio, but on stage they looked poorly choreographed." I acknowledged, with confusion, that creativity and choreography had to be considered separately. It seemed as if creativity, per se, belonged in the studio and choreography on stage. In any case, I realized that creativity and choreography were two very different things; that one should neither consider them as a unit nor use the words interchangeably. Basically, one was a source and the other a skill.

The problem of semantics was posed again when we urged solo choreographers to expand their range by composing for small groups. Once again talented soloists began to bog down. When the dancer created on his own body, there was little need to verbalize or translate the movement. The language between the dancer and the choreographer was a direct one. But once the movement was performed by another, then the verbal mechanism of translating movement became a nightmare.

Nik said, "Choreographing for someone other than oneself was like handing someone a hand full of sand. So much is lost. But you learn to settle for a reasonable percentage."

I shudder to think how much of that initial handful is lost as a dance is handed down to several replacements, or revived a generation later.

Today many of those students are actively choreographing and presenting their works in various performing spaces. Most of them are talented, most of them dance beautifully, but few of them can choreograph as yet.

Until I taught composition I had always equated good choreography with creativity. I know now that this is not the case.

Composition is a skill, a craft which can be taught and learned. Let me consider it in that cold light for a moment. Ideally it is the means and the method to structure creativity. Basically these skills can be used by the genius and the hack alike. When I say choreography I mean basic choreography. Putting together a simple movement. Making a phrase, building a line of action. Knowing a beginning from an ending. The rudiments of structuring a dance.

Dances exist in many forms; they are wedged into operas, they are the routines for children's neighborhood recitals; they are the patterns used in rock dancing that has recently become so popular; they comprise the repertory of dance companies; they are a framework within which a "Star" exhibits himself; they keep the action going on a Broadway stage; they appear wherever there is a call for structured movement. All these dances are choreographed to be learned, rehearsed, and repeated.

There is a mentality and sensibility associated with choreographing that differs from that of creativity. The choreographic process is objective and dealt with externally, whereas creativity is a highly subjective inner process.

The majority of choreographers never venture into themselves for their material. They are content to arrange and rearrange prescribed steps and patterns. If they are fortunate enough to have fine dancers performing the material, the performers' artistry will make up for the choreographer's lack of it.

There are many books on the market about composing, composition, and choreography. They range from do-it-yourself manuals to accounts of the process of great artists.

In the early days of modern dance, before the art had defined itself or the great creators of that time could concern themselves with how they were doing it, being so overwhelmed with the doing of it, Louis Horst supplied a great deal of simple and direct assistance to the profession. Horst was Graham's musical director during her most memorable period. He was a fine pianist and composer, and it stood to reason that he would bring his musical skills and knowledge to the teaching of composition for dance. They included such directives as theme and variation, ABA (sonata) form, counterpoint, and others. Horst reached out and drew from the other arts as well—painting, sculpture, and architecture. Craft is craft, and great craftsmanship is as essential to great choreography as it is to every other art form.

Doris Humphrey, great artist and great mind that she was, also produced a substantial book on dance composition.

Unfortunately, it was assumed by teachers of choreography that the student would supply the creativity, but the methods for getting at creativity other than their own natural talent were few.

I must interject here to answer the question, "Why the need for dancers to choreograph their own dances?" Most musicians do not compose their repertoires, nor do actors write the plays they perform. Why must dancers choreograph? They must for a number of reasons.

Primarily, dancers must dance, and they will do almost anything in order to do so. They will join any choreographer who asks them, not thinking or caring about the choreography as long as there are steps for them to do. Dances cannot be effectively written for the learning, because most dancers do not read a dance notation of any sort. Video recording may remedy this some day, but for now if they cannot dance with a company, they must compose for themselves.

Companies are expensive organizations to maintain. Finances involved in rehearsals and production on any economic level are prohibitive. A million dollars to Ballet Theater is comparable to a thousand to a company living on unemployment insurance.

One can only learn to perform by performing and therefore you need something to perform. These things are called dances, and dances need to be choreographed.

Teachers of choreography exhort their students to be creative, to be more inventive. When that invention is not forthcoming, it is felt the student has neither talent nor choreographic potentiality, or a mediocre one at best. Yes and no. A talented choreographer with creative insight and the right working opportunities could become a great artist. A choreographer without that creativity could range from ingenious to impossible, depending upon his personality and mind.

By the end of the 1950s standard choreographic devices were producing formulaic dances, and the third and fourth generation of dancers were simply following prescribed patterns to produce dances. Seemingly, we had reached a deadend, and some said the modern dance had died.

Then came the deluge, the student revolution of the late 1960s, and no young person was willing to take instructions from anyone. They were going to do their own thing. Discipline and training were too difficult, too boring, and besides, they were taught by people over forty. The young looked for and followed any banner that proclaimed their cause, and what better banner in dance than "Any movement is dance." Had they looked more carefully or listened more intelligently, they would have realized that slogan should have read "Any movement *can be* danced."

The wave of rebellion swept the establishments and a lot of ivy-clad walls came tumbling down. With it fell what was left of the precarious modern dance establishment, the Connecticut College Summer Session for Dance. Only Hanya Holm remained in Colorado Springs. So much was heedlessly washed away in that tide. So much was lost. So many opportunists rushed in with the flood to also do their own thing—not the thing that was called for or necessary to redirect the art; but just what suited them, and what they could get away with, because there was no one to challenge them.

Composition was replaced with permissiveness; permissiveness became the definition of creativity. The art itself was dismembered and served up to feed the therapists, sociologists, psychologists, and the various cults which grew out of the times. Oh sad, sad days.

I walked upon that campus during the session's last years, and was haunted by the spirit of the past that originated in Bennington. I remembered the dancers who once worked there, those fierce spines, those elegant necks, all those pony-tails, and the aura of the priestesses. I remember the work, the fear, the work, the dedication, the work . . . all gone, all gone. So much will have to be rediscovered. What a waste of precious time, so much time will be needed for this rediscovery, and if there is anything a dancer holds most precious and cannot afford to lose, it is time.

The professional choreographer is a special breed of person. When one talks about a choreographer, he is talking about a person who has the stomach and the nervous system to bring a work to the boards. Mounting a work is like mounting an offensive. Logistics—manpower—maneuvers and Maalox.

Many choreographers get the reputation for being bastards. When one is fighting for his life, when one is drowning, he forgets his manners; he hasn't time to cut his nails.

A choreographer must deal with people, personalities, and pressure, all of which drain his energy and time and force him to make quick decisions, and almost always, as curtain-time draws near, there is the squeeze in the last hours when he resigns himself to not getting what he wants to see, but having to see what he's getting.

Choreography is a skill, like surgery. It must be practiced over and over again until the facility becomes innate, second nature. Creativity, on the other hand, operates in such a way that if the same thing is practiced over and over again, it becomes second hand, stale.

Choreography deals with so many external factors, such as: who is dancing the role, whether it is a solo or group piece, what music is used, where on the program the dance appears, the audience involved, rehearsal time, rehearsal space. These demands, even before the choreographic work begins, need professional handling. To avoid much of this, a choreographer tries to maintain his own company so he can practice his skill without the constant harassment of these interruptions, without having to wait for the general director of a company to invite him, on whim, to choreograph. The stability of a dance company offers a choreographer the ability to grow. Resident choreographers know the dancers they are using. Know their bodies, their capabilities, and how to challenge the dancers as well as themselves. Above all, they know they can demand of the performer his responsibility to bring the movement to life.

There is a line in the film *The Turning Point* that made me cringe. It occurred in the part when the young, abstract choreographer insisted the dancer bring no emotion to the movement, "Just do the steps." "Shit," I thought, "what every abstract choreographer wants is that his dancers invest the movement with what the movement requires without the overlay of extraneous emotionalism." A big difference. There are hundreds of qualities with which a dancer can imbue his movement. But a choreographer cannot teach these things in his brief rehearsal time; he must expect his dancers to supply them.

Dancers who "make it," are "naturals." But everyone of those naturals had a choreographer who took the time to clarify what he wanted from them: Ashton's care with Fonteyn, Tudor's with Nora Kaye, and Cranko's with Marcia Haydee.

If a choreographer does not work carefully and over a generous period of time with an artist, only a fraction of the choreography will come to life. Choreographers, generally speaking, do not have that time with one-shot opportunities. Only by having their own company can they make that time, time not only for the dancer to learn a dance properly, but time for the ballet to ripen, to mellow, to be performed before audiences, and allowed to become itself. Who can afford that? Only a large established organization can manage it financially. How long did it take to create "Swan Lake?" And how many times was it performed before it took its final form?

To create is to bring into existence that which did not exist before. Like any birth, conception begins in the body. But unlike a child coming into the world, the artist doesn't know the shape or form of his offspring until it appears. Gestation periods will vary with the character, nature, and the unique identity of the res. It is brought into the world in a number of ways: through the senses or the mind; through the heart or the gut; into the fingers or the eye or the backbone or the legs.

Over the many years a creator learns to channel those new existences, born deep inside himself, into the various parts of his body which then craft or mold his art. The craftsman's skills begin to give visible identity to this intuitive nucleus. This issuance and molding occur both simultaneously and instantaneously.

During this birth, the artist is at his most vulnerable. All of his outward physical strength is suspended as the emerging process begins. He is metamorphosized. He becomes so possessed by this new existence that he must externalize it, or as is so often the case, go mad.

When the birth is completed, the craftsman, who serves as midwife, knows what he must do next, knows what shape and form this creature shall have, knows the structure of this entity. The creator then rests; exhausted, he falls back into himself and the craftsman continues working, calling upon that internal judgment when there are decisions to make.

Some artists are more fertile than others. Mozart's genius passed freely from inside to out. Dickens's gift was bounteous. Picasso's was inexhaustible. Choreographers are not so fortunate; before they can see what they have created, their images must be molded onto their own bodies or onto those of others. Bodies are not always dependable, or tuned and acquiescent as a piano might be for a musician. Bodies are far too susceptible to the erasures and resistances of human frailty, inability, and forgetfulness.

Improvisation is the practice of transporting the seed from its intuitive womb into the hands of the choreographer. Improvisation is the practice of creativity. For dancers it is a way of gaining an understanding of textures, imagery, depth, and motional resonance that can lend a richness and poignancy to performance. It is one of the best trainings and preparations for the art of performing.

Improvisation has a long and flamboyant history. It is a highly developed art among wits and satirists, fertile minds skimming an internal reservoir of imagery, musicians rambling along, cleverly weaving and dodging wherever their quick associations take them.

In dance, I can only write about those periods within recall. How the Greeks danced and what they danced about, I cannot say. The improvisations that were the aftermath of Isadora's freedom, I can remember, alas.

To dance of the free spirit, the free body, of the soul, of mankind, of life, of despair, needed nothing more than a little music, preferably Chopin, and out it poured. Those indulgences in the name of art were wonderfully excessive. They were improvisations executed to get something off the dancer's chest, not out from their creative hatchery.

For the creative artist the geography of this creative source lies a great deal deeper within the recesses of the body. Everyone of us can claim a heritage locked deeply inside ourselves of at least ten thousand years. The body is an incredibly wise and knowledgeable source. Consider then, the limitations and the paucity of experience gained during a lifetime. What would that be? Thirty, forty, fifty years? The layman draws from his limited recent reservoir, but the artist knows how far back and how deeply his tap lines must reach. The body knows a great deal more about the human experience than anyone could possibly learn in a lifetime.

A dancer need only confront his arm and say, "If you know so much about what you want to do, show me." The mechanisms in that arm will timorously surface. At first it will move hesitantly, not knowing how seriously it will be taken. The dancer must at this point show every bit of faith he can muster to allow that limb to operate freely without imposition. All the technical skill and virtuosity of the dancer must be made available to fulfill whatever movement occurs. All the richness within the dancer's command unfolds. In this instantaneous union, the dancer performs the instantaneous choreography he has released from his source. Improvisation reveals the organic development, the inherent natural design of movement that lies deep inside the muscles. When artistry intrudes in this logical flow of action, it disturbs and alters this naturalism to correspond with and reflect the mind-vision of the artist.

There are no rehearsals for this performance. No messages are conveyed. It is the art of dance at its purest, from source to realization. When it is finished, the dance is over, never to be repeated as such again.

Dancers who can bring an improvisation into its fullest revelation experience a creative fulfillment which often misleads them into thinking they have consciously choreographed the dance. Their ambitions exceed what their choreographic skill can support. This is when difficulties arise, but for the aspirant, no more difficult than building a skyscraper with sand. Impossible physically, perhaps, but dreams have surmounted greater obstacles.

Sometimes choreographers find themselves working with creative dancers from whom they draw their initial material. The choreographer might direct the dancer to improvise and then draw still further from him. As the composition continues, it is best that both of them understand their relationship. Their relationship has now become so close and the evolvement of materials so intricately distributed between the two that inevitably a great deal of confusion will arise over who did what. This has often led to animosity and hard feelings.

Some people can create, others can choreograph. The blessed are those few who can do both, and in addition are talented.

Artistry is the x-factor in the formula of creativity. It is, I feel, a particular chemical imbalance in the body that heightens sensation and redirects and diverts the natural course of man's actions in order to devise new statements of man-made naturalisms called art. This chemical is carried through the blood stream as quickly as adrenaline. It bathes the neuro-muscular system and stimulates it to manifest its unique judgments. Where this chemical is lodged, where it is manufactured, what the chemical actually is, I cannot say. It does not feel like an electrical impulse, it feels wet. Perhaps it is generated in some of those deep and as yet unexplored recesses of the brain or in the gut or in the lining of the abdominal walls. All of these areas seem to feel the strain acutely. This is hardly a scientific explanation, but this is what it feels like to me.

It would be a wonderfully insane indulgence to say why people choreograph and how they choreograph. But I do feel safe in tracing the course. An artist draws forth from himself a new life and then proceeds to give it form, so that a dancer can reveal it to an audience. If artistry is involved, then he has also contributed to the furtherance of his art.

I wonder, too, if audiences know how much great art they miss by not attending rehearsals. But what audiences do know is the miracle that occurs when everything mixes properly. They know the melting rapture that sweeps from the stage or rehearsal area to ravish those parts within us we cannot protect from beauty.

How does one talk about this? How do dancers ever learn? But they do.

Washington, D.C.
New York City

Light Vs. Lighting

I think that I have spent as much time over the years standing on stage, lighting a show, as I've spent on stage performing. That's a lot of time. That's a lot of standing. Standing still, walking through areas, holding costumes, and waiting. You think about a lot of things when you wait.

Waiting to be lit is one of the aging processes built into touring. Bad food is another. Standing on cold and dirty stages as you feel your muscles tighten and your spirit drain from your body probably has convinced more dancers to leave the profession than a short Achilles' tendon. The crazy thing about all this is that the dancer usually has no idea what the lighting looks like. He has no idea what is seen from out front. All he knows, and for that matter, cares about, is what light is provided for him to see his way about the stage.

You have to psyche yourself very carefully when you light, because you're dealing with technicians, people who operate on a very different energy level than the dancer. That's the first thing you notice and must resolve—the different urgencies that exist backstage. In the beginning you fight it. You get angry with people plodding about. You can't imagine how insensitive some of the people who work backstage can be. The dancer faces unnecessary obstacles in the wings making exits treacherous, drafts, no heat, dirt, cigarette butts, loud mouths, and so on. Unless the theater has a good "tech" director and a good stage manager, it can be hell, but after a while your survival techniques take over and you join it. You suspend yourself and drop out. You learn to wait. You can get a lot of reading or knitting done during those hours, but mostly you think.

I think about what sort of dances I can create with only one light cue. I think about never having to tour again, never having to set-up and never having to light the same damn program again.

I think about my predecessors, the early Greek performers, who sought the brightest part of the day in which to perform, as well as outdoor stages, while I wait until darkness and work indoors. I think of how they operated with one spotlight, the sun, while I often use a hundred or more lamps. I think about how far and how complexly the dance has evolved since its earliest formative years. In the beginning there was only the beauty that nature provided, but then, as man developed and grew restless and became impatient with nature, he created his own methods for making beauty—artificial methods—and called them art.

But as I stand on the stage, holding a Helenca costume, on a stage in a theater complex in Anywhere, U.S.A., surrounded by lights and wires, projectors and switchboards, walkie-talkies and intercoms, cue sheets, and stop watches, little sparks of nature still ignite to assure me that I'm alive. I can feel my body adapting itself to survival.

The story of life has to do with heat and light and the living cell, and lighting onstage also has to do with heat and light and the human skin. Of late, I've discovered that instead of getting simpler, the closer we get to the source of life and nature the more complicated things become. Answers seem to breed anxiety; maybe we know too much.

We're stopping again, but no one can leave the stage area. It seems the downstage left pool wasn't focused correctly. It won't take a minute. That means at least fifteen minutes. The light pipe cannot be lowered easily, which means the big ladder must be brought on stage and two stagehands have to brace it while one goes up to refocus the lamp. If the stage weren't so dirty, I'd lie down. To hell with it, I'll lie down anyway. I'm sure it was easier in the old days.

Light is what the dancer looks for onstage; lighting is what the audience sees. The dancer responds physically to light while the audience responds artistically to lighting.

The whole idea of lighting has become very complicated today. Stage lighting and especially dance lighting will never be the same since Nikolais; and dancers, whether they like it or not, must learn how to perform in light.

Nik evolved a concept of isolating and lighting the dance figure. He disregarded the traditional past, which was oriented towards naturalism and overhead lighting, and instead lit the dancer so that he was lifted from the stage floor and pulled from the back wall, making him central and dominant.

Although the audience watches a dancer when he walks onstage, there are many things they don't see. One of these things is how the dancer handles the light around him, the stage light. There is also no other place where a dancer can learn how to handle himself in stage light except in performance. Rehearsals don't really count because you can stop and make corrections. In performance, mistakes count. As a matter of fact, rehearsing in a well-lit rehearsal studio may soon be a distinct disadvantage to the dancer because it is wholly unrelated to what he will find onstage.

The first thing he discovers is that certain lighting can jeopardize his foot contact with the floor. Lighting designers try as much as possible to light the dancer and not the floor, and in order to reduce light from "bouncing" or reflecting from the floor, the stages are being covered in darker and darker materials. The closest thing to terror I know is dancing on the dark. The only approximation I know of the sensation of leaping onto an unlit black Marley floor is the fear the fifteenth-century sailor had of falling off the ends of a flat earth.

Another nightmare a dancer must build resistance to is "klieg" or blinding light concentration from side lighting. This can push or pull the strongest technician from his balance. A strong klieg can hook into the dancer's eyeball from the side and yank him over.

When dancers perform they set their head so they either look or appear to look out. But automatically their vision includes the floor and the stage boundaries. They can see where they are going to step and where they are going to land, and if they can't, they tighten up. They often spot on the floor for balance; if the floor is invisible, then panic sets in.

This is why dancers are like moths. They will always gravitate to light. They are also like humans—they step out of light if it is too hot. Unless, of course, they are mad Englishmen, or it's freezing onstage.

Talking about freezing, I wonder what became of those lighting unitards Betty gave the company for Christmas some years ago. Too often the dancers had to "show some skin" when the temperature was low, and Betty Young ordered a set of flesh colored hand-knitted woolen outfits for all of us to wear during lighting. They were a Godsend when we lit the "nudie" dances. I guess we hit so many cold stages we must have worn them out. You see, the backstage mentality is such that, during lighting sessions, where there is no one performing, there is no need to clean or heat the stage. They have absolutely no understanding of the time it takes to warm and limber muscles. The only muscular skill I've ever seen stagehands display is keeping their trousers up under their beer-bellies. I don't know how they do it.

A professional dancer develops a sensitivity to light intensity. They can feel the "hot spot" (center) of a spotlight. They know when they are lit. But if for some reason the concerted effort of ten backstage technicians fails to bring up the lights, then he must also make dancing in the dark convincing.

What the lighting designer and the audience see is what is illuminated on the stage. What the dancer looks at are rows of blinding lights.

There we go again. We've been told we're a little behind schedule. We're going to push things along, and that everything looks beautiful up to now. I wonder if anyone noticed that the ladder is still onstage? Are the stagehands taking a break now? Aw, the hell with it. What was I thinking about?

A lighting designer usually tries to make a luminous narrative occur. Lights come up—areas feed in—spots fade in and out—pools isolate a single figure—silhouettes emphasize a sculptural pattern—and other devices give eloquence to the stage space.

The choreographer understands and goes along with this. But if, for some all-too-recurring reason, a technician brings up a higher or lower reading on any of his dimmers, no one understands what havoc this plays upon the performer's already strained temperament. Rarely have I gone through a performance when all the lighting has worked, and never have I gone on stage expecting it to. Making stage adjustments is so second nature to me that I hardly realize I'm doing it. It has become part of my performing technique.

When I rehearse a dance in a studio, I relish it. Because I know once I am on the stage I will have the fear and worry that the lighting inconsistencies will turn my muscle tone into muscle tension. Once a dancer is onstage he is helpless. If something goes wrong, he can say nothing, only groan inwardly. His only voice is the stage manager's in the wings. The performer is completely at his mercy.

During a performance of "Hoopla" the spotlight went off. In that particular solo, the spot played an important part. After the performance, Tony, my stage manager, was impressed that I continued dancing and changed none of the choreography. "I knew you were watching me, Tony, and would do something about the missing light," I said. And he did. I often look offstage during a concert to assure myself that I am not alone, that my stage manager is with me. Without him, I am adrift.

Sometimes a lighting mistake can have a happy ending. One season at the Beacon Theater, at the premiere of "Déjà Vu," a solo in five parts, I entered for the fourth section. The light in the area in which I was going to begin the dance was insufficient. I looked offstage to my stage manager, pointed distinctly to the spot I was to enter into and mouthed off the stage to him—"light." I'd never done that before and he couldn't believe his eyes. He hastily called for more light and a spot at the opposite end of the stage came up. The audience laughed. I pointed again, and the spot went out and boom—lights came on. The audience laughed again. I shrugged and, not daring to kill a good thing, walked to my mark and started the dance. Afterward we added more light to that cue. But the ham in me kept the opening play with the lights in the act.

The dancer rarely knows what the total picture of the stage looks like, but he can see light and color. Blues and steels are cools. They can turn a blue-toned skin to an unearthly alabaster. Walking onto a blue stage during lighting, Margot Fonteyn stopped dead, walked downstage, and in a pleading voice asked, "May I have a little pink please?" Whether or not she got it in performance I cannot say, but she was promised it. She accepted that promise. Trusting soul. Not me. I want to see what I'm getting before I go on. I don't trust my hairy white body with anyone.

If you want to see Michael Ballard come to life, throw a green light on him and he'll thrash until the color is changed.

It is in the inherent nature of the human body to respond to light, heat, and color. All three factors cause stimulation to the most rudimentary of organisms. In spite of the mechanical sophistication of contemporary stage-craft, nature still plays her role at a dance performance because the dancer is still a natural instrument. He may be clothed, lit, and accompanied by artificially made materials, but he still remains basically a living organism.

The dancer's response to light and color is different from the lighting designer and the audience. The body is the only living instrument used to make art, and unfortunately we rarely think about art in the making. Art always seems to be an end product.

Performance is art in the making.

Performance allows nature to get into the art.

These are some of the things you think about while you stand around waiting to be lit.

London, England

On Nikolais

Introduction

I met Alwin Nikolais thirty years ago during a dance summer session at Colorado College. I had been discharged the previous year from the navy, and after a period of working road company musicals and an unmentionable night club stint, I was on my way back to New York to continue a career in Broadway musicals. I was all of twenty-two and undecided about my eventual career. Having the temperament and mind that I do, I was looking for a career with vision. And vision I got indeed during that inspiring summer with Nik. So filled was I with the endless possibilities of the art, my concern then became whether I would have enough time in my life to do all the things in dance I could now envision and conceive.

I returned with Nik to become a student at the Henry Street Playhouse in New York City, where he had recently been made a co-director. I had first to spend time unlearning, and then learning. Then, after many years, we became colleagues.

In my long and widely traveled career, he is the only genius I have ever met, much less known.

His is too great a life to write about briefly. These, however, are some thoughts.

Opening

For most people, Alwin Nikolais is a mystery. Although there has been a great deal written about his stage work, there are no "little stories" to tell about him. He has no cult, no coterie. He rarely goes out in New York, but instead entertains a great deal at home. He has played to great and wide audiences; abroad he is a household word. He is the foremost international artist in dance from America; still he is a mystery.

Since he doesn't appear in his productions, his audiences do not know what to expect in the way of his appearance, so that at the end of a performance when he does appear, his reception is greeted with a roar from the audience that raises the roof. For here, at last, is the reality behind the magic. Perhaps that is what makes him appear so formidable—his magic.

In reality he is remarkably available.

He is called magician, wizard, genius, and genius he is indeed; for among other things, he has generated the most original thinking and analysis of dance in this generation, as well as changed the visual look of the American stage. He took the theater art, which had become fractioned into painting, music, dance, and poetry—and was now pursuing the course of a dramatic art—and pulled the pieces together to make a twentieth-century theater art—a theater art of abstraction.

Nikolais was born in Southington, Connecticut, and christened Alwin Theodore; but to presidents and first ladies, emperors and empresses, and the thousands of students who have crossed his path, he is known as Nik.

His credo is oriented solely towards his art. He is a relentless worker. His life is spent on very little other than his work. His art portrays one picture of the man, while his personal life paints a very different visage. He sees his art as something he must do, and sees himself as the means for doing it.

When people ask me to talk about Nikolais, I often find myself at a loss for words; for to me, who probably knows him more intimately than anyone else in the world, he often remains a mystery still.

Although Nik was a product of earlier values, he is today a statement of the future.

Those earlier days of modern dance may have been hampered by many things, but what carried it through so much of its marvelous growth was the intimacy of the class size. At the Henry Street Playhouse, we had two studios. The larger could handle fifteen dancers and the smaller ten. If there were more than twenty-five people in class, including the company, we would join forces and use the stage if it were available to us. Today, all of that studio space would fit into our large studio alone, and a class of less than forty students seems unattended.

After warm-ups and pliés, Nik would go to the piano and accompany the class as we went across the floor. And could he play. I mean, Sweet Jesus could he play. And did we dance our asses off. We all lived for that hour of going across the floor. After class it was not perspiration that poured from our bodies; it was exhilaration.

Over the years it has been an abiding teaching principle with me that after all is said and done, when I come into the home stretch of a class there is to be no more talk, no more explanation, no more teaching; it is all stops out and clear sailing to the finish line. That is one of Nik's legacies to my teaching.

Decentralization

Classical ballet training is, for the most part, the major dance training in this country, and practically the only training in Europe. It is a centralized technique. Placement is very often inflexible. Not only is it ground into the dancer, but out of necessity dancers themselves hang onto it for technical security.

The women have a better time of it than the men, because when supported they are free to use their torsos in a less centered manner. But the men, for whom the classical vocabulary consists predominantly of turns with leg and air variations, are rarely challenged off their center.

When the modern dance first sought its movement distinctions in the 1930s, it investigated new areas of movement that often were in direct contrast with the ballet vocabulary. Where the ballet took to the air, the modern dance took to the floor level. Pelvic action was emphasized, making the spine less rigid, and tilted action helped take the dancer off his vertical.

It is inevitable that any pattern of movement, ballet or modern, if repeated enough times, will centralize itself in the security mechanisms of the body.

Nik came to this challenge of rigidity with his concept of decentralization, that basically dealt with creating a fluid center. He did this through improvisation, and a technical approach to movement that included fluidity of mind, imagery, and response. He found it was necessary to decentralize the psyche as well as the body.

Moving the center to any part of the body necessitated an unusually quick and direct thinking. These shifts prevented the energy from becoming rooted. They also brought into prominence parts of the body (chest, hips, back) other than the extremities. The resulting movement seemed unpredictable and rhythmically complex. One wondered how the dancer could remember the intricacy of the choreography based on this new method. But once the ability to create a flexible psyche as well as spine was incorporated into the technical training, it was not difficult for a dancer to expand his vocabulary enormously. Vitality and quick thinking are parts of any good dancer's make-up.

One of Nik's most difficult tasks in class was to knock the hardness of self out of the dancer and replace it with a fluid selflessness. To achieve this, he asked from the dancer a floating concentration and a malleable placement. *Decentralization* was what he called this practice to gain motional mobility as well as freedom from egocentricity. One could now train to develop not just parts of the whole, but the whole part.

As students in those days, we were not the ideal raw material upon whom an innovator of his calibre could evolve and shape theories. As a matter of fact we were a pretty motley crew. Most of us had little in common with each other, apart from our absolute devotion to Nik. What made the chemistry work in those years was that he called upon us to contribute to, not simply take class. He made it clear to us that he had to see us do what he was calling for before he could see where he was going next. And did we work. Gladys, Phyllis, Dorothy, Bill, Beverly, Coral, and myself. We were black and white, tall and short, nervous and sedated, heavy and thin, wiry and phlegmatic, but we all had a common focus: Nik.

On thinking back, I realize now how our diversity was probably the best thing that could have happened to him. I mean the odds were with him. With this cross-section someone was bound to understand what he was saying, because once one of us materialized what he wanted, then we all knew what he wanted of us, and we put out.

Movement and Motion

I would say one of the first major concepts Nik dealt with was his distinction between movement and motion. "Movement is the gross or general pattern of action, and motion the inner itinerary that qualifies it and distinguishes it as dance. All creatures, human and otherwise, move; but anyone who can apply their sentient facilities towards sensing the motion transpiring through their movement, dances."

Previously dancers had followed the actor's training and primarily had given their actions emotional motivation. But with this new definition of motion, he brought to dance its own motivational basis. Motion. This, of course, did not preclude the emotional coloration a performer could bring to his performance, if he so chose, but it did give the dancer the means to fulfill abstraction and pursue the course of nonverbal and nonliteral dance. The whole gamut of sentient experience became part of the dancer's vocabulary. By using motion as the common denominator, the double meaning of abstraction was made clear: 1. to distill to essence, and 2. nonverbal, sentient.

Theory and application particularly in art can often stand poles apart. It is a tribute to his greatness as a teacher that he could impart this theory of motional motivation to the thousands who have worked with him over the years.

Perhaps the greatest tribute I can recall was, after years of listening to and reading the constant carping at Nikolais's "abstract theories," and "dehumanization," I entered a dance room in a public school in Columbus, Ohio and there written on a border surrounding the room were the words, "Space," "Shape," "Time," and "Motion." These youngsters were learning about dance in its own terms, not borrowing those of the musician, or actor, or writer. I was genuinely touched. I couldn't help but think back to those anguished early years, when as students we struggled to understand and gain the skill to replace emotional fervor with motional passion, as measured by dynamic intensity and fervor. Of course, the ability to achieve this metamorphosis from movement to motion still rested with the dancer and his performing artistry. Through his capacity to bring movement to life, to its motional identity and legibility, he could communicate in the abstract to an audience. Once he achieved this, the dancer could then perform an abstract narrative without imposing a story line upon its structure.

At the Playhouse, in those early days, all we wanted to do was what we called dance, which meant "shaking our asses." We were not a technically proficient group, because we were all very young and with little prior training. Phyllis was sixteen years old when I joined them, and I was the old man at twenty-two. It took Nik years to make us see through movement and discover dance. It made of us all unique stylists; yet when we performed his material our ensemble was incredible, or as it was so lyrically described by the press at that time, dehumanized.

By learning to identify motion, we sealed our individual bond with the art of dance, because now we knew what dancing meant for ourselves. We would never need to wear someone else's shoes, nor need to follow in the footprints made by someone else's feet.

What He Teaches and What He Creates

Perhaps the best way to know Nik is to be able to make the distinction between his work as a teacher-philosopher and the man who created an abstract theater. He is many men.

With an artist like Graham, for example, whose technical approach to movement was so closely incorporated into her choreography, it was not difficult to know what she taught from what one saw on stage. This is not the case with Nik. It is natural for the general audience seeing his work onstage to think that this is what he practices in the classroom, since this is the case with most every other choreographer.

What is done onstage is his personal vision. He shares this only with his audience. He imparts none of this to his students. Onstage he creates theater; in class he teaches dance. His approach to dance in the classroom is of classical purity. His insistence on motional revelation and the clarity of articulation is relentless.

I can remember clearly the endless classes he taught just on the principles of walking. The lifting of the leg, the rotary action of the thigh to introduce the leg to forward. The placement of the hip and weight, the shifting of the body as a unit over the forward foot. The clear seeing eye. The open chest. The awareness of passing through space. The continuity of an uninterrupted flow of energy. The care to sustain a level of action. The care not to intrude into the sideward plane or the high or low levels.

Of course this analysis of movement evolved directly from the pedagogic insight of Hanya Holm. She created so solid a basis of movement analysis that it allowed Nik to go on and break new ground and take the next step. He is honored to feel himself a continuation of that great lady. He worked with Hanya as her assistant for about five years, more than twenty-five years ago. Today they still work together at our school.

His choreographic and stage visions, on the other hand, deal with the multiple complexity of theater. The energies and dynamics of motion, light, color, sound, sculpture, architecture, design, and voice, all become part of his creative pallette.

To the studio he brought a definition of principles to extend the vocabulary of the profession. Through movement analysis, through insights which defined the creative process, through the orientation of improvisation, through concepts of totality, identity, sentient participation, decentralization, immediacy, and many other definitions that made the art lucid. It all seemed so natural because they fit like essential pieces into the fabric of dance, and thousands of his students quickly took them and absorbed them into the mainstream of dance without realizing the source.

Nikolais is a source as well as a sorcerer.

Audiences

I said to him one day, "Do you realize you don't depend upon a cult or a coterie? How do you expect to be a success?"

"Yep," he answered, "But, I have an audience."

I don't believe there is another artist involved with theater today who knows audiences as Nik does. Most choreographers who attend performances of their own work usually remain backstage; it's safer there. Occasionally, some will sit out front—it's not that they can't abide seeing their work so frequently —it's simply because they are helpless when they cannot contribute to the stage action once the curtain has gone up. The performance is entirely out of their hands, and this frustration hurts, sometimes physically so.

With Nik it is different. He has found a way to remain a part of his productions. He does this as part of the audience. Sitting in the back of the house with direct inter-communication to his stage manager backstage, he starts the house lights down when he feels the audience is settled. He sets the overture levels to match the audience's pre-curtain hub-bub. He keeps his finger on the audience's pulse throughout the entire performance. He adjusts lights when it becomes necessary and important. (This becomes a god-send to his stage manager who must set up and light a show in as many as three or four different houses a week throughout a tour.) Audience reaction, the direct response during the performance, is the only criticism to which he'll respond.

He said to me once, "Do you know there are several movements in 'Noumenon' (Mobiles) which have drawn specific responses in every theater I have seen it played throughout the world?" That means in the Orient, Africa, Europe, South America, and the U.S. "But what is more remarkable is that the tonal pitch of response is always the same. Everyone says that dance is the universal language, but that's not totally true. It is more universal than other arts perhaps, but I feel now that while it is possible for people of different cultures to respond alike, it occurs through abstraction. It occurs in that unguarded moment when they are sensing it before they can think about it."

Audiences change, artists grow. Audiences are fickle and have current interest; artists have continuity. Some choreographers will deliberately ignore their audiences. Some won't admit their concern. I, for example, know how I would like them to respond and consider that response. But no one is as knowledgeable and concerned with his audience as is Nik. They are an essential part of the theater and he takes them seriously. He does not play games with them or treat them contemptuously. Except on rare occasions, he is part of them every night.

He sees a direct line between the stage and the audience and is wary and distrustful of those inevitable middle men such as producers, managers, committees, boards, unions, and press, who often stand in the path of that direct link.

"How did it go tonight? " I'll ask.

"The audience liked it."

The first time I saw a Nikolais production was in 1972. I had danced in everything he'd choreographed since 1949, and left his company twenty years later in 1969. For the following three years I was never in New York City when he was giving his seasons; but in 1972 at his Broadway season at the ANTA theater, I sat out front and watched his work for the first time.

In all honesty, I had no idea of what that total stage looked like when I was dancing his pieces. I was staggered, simply staggered. It created a world so completely of its own that for a moment I felt I didn't know the man who had created it. I knew some of those dances inside out, having danced them myself for years, but to see them now with his eyes I found myself without any frame of reference. I was lifted, I was transported, I transcended. Suddenly I was in awe of him, and this time I saw him objectively, for the genius he is.

Emotion and Emotional

Abstraction is too difficult a word to define fully. It generally connotes images of all sorts of heartless implications. It paints a world coldly ruled by numbers and angles, which fall like ice water on the flame of emotional turmoil. It is not as easy to grasp as a good story line. The viewer is called upon to participate, which is always an inconvenience, and when that participation is not forthcoming, the charge of "incoherence" is raised. On the other hand it can provide a perfect cover-up for inability.

Abstraction and realism in art squared off in the mid-1950s. Jackson Pollack had torn the lid off the definition of painting, and other powerful artists were rampaging across the whole art scene. Abstraction was here to stay.

Approaches to aesthetic response differ. With realism the brain can tell the senses what they have felt; with abstraction the senses can stimulate the brain into non-literal imagery. Nikolais's art operates through the latter. This is the path abstraction takes toward communication. One would have a difficult time entering his world through the literal brain. One experiences his world abstractly, through the senses: optic, aural, and kinetic.

His audiences must not have exhausted or lost their ability to wonder. To marvel at concept. To respect supersonics. To be plain thankful for the telephone and to feel humbled by the power of their own sensory equipment, for their sentient scope.

Many years ago, Nik choreographed a piece called "Prism" (1956). It dealt with some of his earliest efforts to fraction movement through light and color. The finale embodied some of his most relentless choreography. It started with running and just built and built until the momentum gathered enough force for us to run up and across the plaster cyclorama at the Henry Street Playhouse. As we reached this energy peak, we all turned from upstage, faced the audience and with the same speed rushed downstage towards them. As we reached the footlights a battery of photo flashlights aimed at the audience went off. In that blinding moment the curtain lowered quickly, erasing from the audience's eye the energy hurtling towards them.

Well, talk about gasps and screams. It was indeed a powerful moment in sensory response.

Afterward a woman came backstage, wild-eyed and gasping, clutching everyone in sight and breathless with praise. But when she came to Nik, after complimenting him she told him it lacked only one thing to make the work complete for her, an "emotional reaction." What made me listen further was I had thought I heard her say "emotional orgasm."

I was taken aback. There she stood emotionally exhausted, quivering, eyes still rolling, and she claimed to have had no emotional reaction. "Look at you," I said, "you're an emotional wreck. What more could you want?"

"Something to tear me apart."

I admired her because she was frank and knew what she looked for on the stage.

Emotion, I realized, was very different from "getting emotional." In any case "getting emotional" is not Nik's objective on stage; his concern is motional qualification (although, in 1971 he created "Scenario," the premise being excessive emotionalism).

I danced in every Nikolais production from 1949 to 1969, and being a dancer with a great and varied emotional range, I brought to every role the emotional balance necessary to fulfill the roles I danced. Emotion reveals itself through a great range of qualities: lightness, hardness, whip, fullness, breath, among countless others. Through these passions, I invested my roles with an emotional intensity. In order to bring abstraction to life, it is essential that the performer achieve the level of motional passion necessary to arrive at totality of gesture. I would burn through the space around me to make time stop. I would lift an arm with a different nuance if it was bathed in green light or red light or in silhouette or side lit, because Nik's art was based on the communicative difference that existed as environments changed.

Certainly, I didn't perform the emotions of boy meets girl when I danced the duet from "Kaleidoscope" with Gladys Bailin. I played it with the cool sensuality called for by the austerity of its design. The dance included a long white pole which always united us. It had an Oriental calm. Our make-up split our faces into two colors and we wore a headpiece which extended our cranial bone structure; our costumes were full tights. For Gladys and me, the dance was about two people on a long journey, perhaps through life. It was a very stirring duet accompanied by a lovely flute melody.

But this was in 1956, when dancing in full-body tights was not common practice in modern dance. Men danced in men's clothes and women in dresses or skirts; otherwise it was difficult to get "emotional" about them. Seeing the human form revealed in tights gave you two choices; you could either think dirty or come to grips with dance as abstraction—a very difficult choice I might add.

The first critiques viewed it in the Freudian jargon so common in that day. When this didn't make sense, they took to "dehumanize," and "out of this world," which made about as much sense.

Nik is not a Freudian. Freud sought a part, Nik sought the total. Freud made sexuality a major motivation; Nik tried to put it into balance with other factors.

Unless you were there, it is difficult to understand the household influence Freud wielded in the 1930s and 1940s. It wasn't safe to love your parents without drawing suspicion to your motives. Innocence was no excuse for the number of phallic symbols one had lying about the house.

It was almost like a symbolistic reign of terror. A dream about a shoelace was enough to commit you, and if you liked bananas, well everyone knew what that meant. Of course, when it came to this extreme it no longer had anything to do with Freud. His name had become synonymous with dream interpretations, and eventually he himself became a symbol.

"Among other things I was not a Freudian because I objected to the interpretive vocabulary of fetal, fertile, and phallic. I know Freud had a vision greater than what he was made to represent. Perhaps it is what he is made to represent that I disagree with. The totality of Gestalt psychology better represents my thinking."

I don't think Nik could ever have gotten his philosophy and thinking off the ground if he had not channeled it through improvisation. Improvisation had come a long way from its early days of permissiveness and an even longer way in its direction and sophistication.

In Wigman's classes dancers improvised and that was that. You did it and then you sat down and very little, if anything, was said.

As Hanya developed this area, they were called Class Lessons. Hanya set the premise and looked to see that it was made evident and inventive. She never permitted indulgence, and when she saw it or sensed it was about to happen, like a cat twitching its tail, she would begin to fiddle with the tip of her braid, which usually at Colorado College had a flower entwined in it.

Nik called his improvisation classes "Theory" and presented them as instant concept, instant choreography, and instant performance. He was looking for the fulfillment, balance, and consonance of these three areas. What better way for dancers to get at abstract communication than to practice it daily in class.

Through these classes it was very easy for all of us to see how personal turmoil and emotionalism intruded to cloud and obscure a gesture. It was also easy to see what physical mannerisms obstructed and limited the doing as well. It made us work harder because we knew what we were working to correct in our own abilities. We could see it in each other and applied it to ourselves.

Sexism

Nik dealt with the subject of male and female behaviorism when for the *Encyclopedia of Sexual Behavior* (1961) he wrote a lengthy article which dealt primarily with sexist role-playing in dance. As a dance teacher, he often came up against the brick wall of the manners and mannerisms prescribed by social mores. He hammered away at the women who retreated behind Victorian frailty and ruthlessly imitated the male machismo. Before he could teach decentralization, he had to strip the dancer of his sexist cover.

In his abstract expressionist theater, the men and women wore the same costumes and freely interchanged roles. I remember he often used dynamic Coral Martindale as one of the "men," without giving a second thought to what role she should be playing because she was a "female." With the exception of lifts and other acts requiring certain strengths, he used all his dancers interchangeably.

He also insisted that on stage his artists rise above the erogenous, and that we not carry our beds onto the boards.

But it would be misleading to imply that Nik ignored sexuality. He was one of the first to present nude dancers on national public television. In "Relay," a made-for-television film produced by the BBC in London, he utilized the naked human form to create a particular effect. When it was televised in the U.S. it was X-rated.

In Japan, the Associated Press pondered why Nik wasn't behind bars. A performance of one of his works innocently violated Japanese law when the dancers showed pubic hair on stage. Fortunately, the Japanese police accepted Nik's aesthetics, and he managed to stay out of jail.

The Sense of Consonance

No one has read Nik's book as yet. Much of it sits in first draft form. It is divided into four parts. The first section has been edited many times, but it is still not to his liking. He has stopped working on it mostly because the demands on his time have drawn him to every part of the world, and it just isn't possible to get his mind back to it.

But what a gold mine sits there in first draft.

The first time I read the book I was profoundly taken with one particular insight concerning human behavior. Since dance is a form of human behavior, anything that effects behavior effects dancing.

In dealing with the sensory processes of the body, processes which deal with artistry, he wrote about how far we have come from the limited Aristotelian thinking of the five senses. The dance artist, who personifies the sentient being, trains and develops to sense everything he does; the sense of height when in relevé, of width when in second. Sensing lightness, heaviness, etc., until the conditions of movement become so numerous the word "sensing" gradually replaces "sense of," and eventually the whole sentient realm becomes the ballpark.

At first he brought sentient participation into the dancer's technical training, and gradually through improvisation classes, it found its way into composition as well.

"There is," he wrote, "a sense of consonance present in animal behavior, a sense that finds the internal and external balance for the thing done, a sense that can direct both the Bower bird and the choreographer in building their structures. It is an intuitive judgment which the dancer employs to achieve artistry. When movement is brought into such balance it reveals itself and manifests its Gestalt. It is this identity that communicates abstraction." But he did not leave it at that. He did not theorize and run. He evolved the means for the dancer to find this balance, and he turned out some fine artists. At least, I've never complained.

It gives, I feel, a misleading impression to readers to read only about conclusions at which a great mind arrives and not about the extensive research and experimentation that resulted in those conclusions. Certainly, Madame Curie did not pull a packaged vial of radium from her cupboard and tell the world it had been sitting there for fifteen years. The troubled and dedicated story of her life is not about radium but instead about the need to know and the strength to fulfill that need. It is to the reader's advantage to relive some of the anguish which precedes a rewarding arrival.

None of these conclusions came easily to Nik. He was thwarted and hampered by many people, and it hurt particularly when it came from people who should have known better. I say this because it was I who responded to the malice more than he did. I realize now why idealists are always looking up: they don't have to see what their feet are standing in.

His decision in those early days to withdraw from the back-biting that dominated the dance scene was a decision made by a mature mind. He had already fulfilled two stages of his career, one before the war in Hartford with a company and school, and a second after the war with Hanya Holm and New York City.

He had choreographed, created a method of dance notation called Choroscript, was an accomplished musician and percussionist, danced (and was a fine dancer), directed a puppet theater, worked with children, and could administrate. More important, he could work with administrators as well. He knew stage craft, design, lighting, costumes, and had also done some acting. It was time to put these together and understand what they all held in common. These were the basis for his total theater. In class "total" was employed as "totality."

It was no small or easy task getting totality from his company. In the first place most of us were too busy growing up and dealing with the pleasures of our own Freudian problems. But somehow he managed to get the ball rolling, and triggered us to do successful things which gave us the courage and an inkling of what he was looking for. We all had then the extraordinary virtue of being good students, to do what we were told to do.

For myself I discovered that practicing totality exclusively in class was impossible, it had to be employed in daily living as well, which brought about the concept of the art ethic and the living ethic and how they interrelated. This in turn introduced such words as morality, honor, grace (not graceful), religion, the soul, God, all of which were impossible to deal with while I was struggling to keep my hips in place as I practiced pliés.

The Vantage Point for Viewing

There is very little middle ground with Nik. He relates directly. There is a direct link between his youth in a small town and his vision of the universe. Although he was a child then, I don't believe he ever had a childhood; certainly in the thirty years I've known him, I have never seen him appear anything other than august. A lonely youth, made even lonelier by the responsibilities forced upon him by the depression, he had that peculiar insight that makes certain children worldly. They are able to see through and into events, rather than simply look at them. I recognized that look, having worked with children for many years. It belongs to someone who, for whatever reasons, is past seeing the world, but well on their way to being part of it.

That is why I say there is no middle ground for Nik. No rudiments. He just took off and for those of us who orbited with him, for those of us who watched him spin his web, it was like riding a shuttle daily from here to some place out there.

If we could only place ourselves out there and look not further out, but back to earth, to man, and at the larger picture of man moving through his environment, we would see what Nikolais had always intended for us to see. It was not to see the world from a point on earth looking out, but to place his audience out there to look back and see the earth as a microcosm.

A viewing seat from the edge of the moon plays upon a very different set of human sensory responses and is, indeed, a far cry from two-on-the-aisle.

For many years I agonized as I read a struggling and searching press trying to grasp, if they tried to grasp—or deal with, if they tried to deal with—his larger spatial concept in terms other than those suggesting a scenario for a Buck Rogers film.

Why should his increasing audiences see his vision and not the press? What was ever going to shock them from their shells?

Then one day it happened.

On July 20, 1969 in the ancient Roman ruins of Baalbeck, Lebanon, we performed "Tent," one of Nik's most ravishing works. Above, the full moon illuminated everything. That great silver ball above was reflected by many smaller silver balls on stage. Electronic music, twentieth-century optics, dancers moving in a new vocabulary of motion, and the desert surrounded us. The desert where at night one wrapped himself, not to stay warm, but to make it bearable to stay cold. The desert at night where in the chilling clarity one discovers the sanity in madness. In that ancient desert looking up to that celestial silver ball, a man walked. A man walked on the moon and nothing on earth would ever be the same again.

That, I thought, should crack open a few bi-valvular minds.

Nik

Nik is an extraordinary cook. I mean he's fabulous. Dinner parties at his place are something else. Not only does he feast the eye and mind, but he can ravish the palate as well. Although I enjoy eating, I stop anywhere in the meal when my stomach is full. "There's no reason not to have more," he'll chastise, "there's nothing fattening in this meal, there are no carbohydrates." But I'm never convinced as I stare down at those pounds of protein.

Preparing dinner for him is a miniature production. All aspects, from shopping through preparation to dining, are taken with great seriousness. The vegetables, the wines, the sauces—everything gets the Nikolais treatment.

Preparing food and swimming in Peconic Bay are the only times he can or ever does relax. Jovial as he appears, he is never without tension, nor can he stop working. He has often made me ponder the fine line between the driven and the dedicated.

His new home has brought more pleasure to him than anything I can think of in years. He has a carpentry workshop and lots of space in which to put the things he makes. He is currently at work on a chandelier which will dwarf the eight and one-half-foot circular table he has already completed, which in turn dwarfs everyone seated around it.

He is big boned and has heft. He cannot be confined and needs space, and if he can't get space, he'll settle for grandeur.

I think it must be the Russian in him that wants to put the emerald on the diamond on the ruby on the sapphire to make room for the pearl. But other than that he is a simple Connecticut Yankee, small town boy, standing on the moon, watching earthlings.

New York City

On Photos and Photographers

Dancers have a mechanism in their heads which lets them know how they appear while they're dancing. It's really quite unreliable and never looks anything like what the audience sees. Nevertheless, they continue to think they know how they appear onstage. Not until they see photographs of themselves will they concede that their shoulders may have been lifted or the line of the arm was broken at the wrist. One has to have a staggering confidence indeed to look at a photograph and say, "You lie." However, dancers can do it.

Photos are the Ombudsmen of performing. They are brutally frank, and if one tries to hoak them up, they become brutally phony.

No one can capture and portray a dancer with words. Words create a mystique perhaps, but only photos can give a form to a name. What would anyone know of Duncan, Wigman, Pavlova, or Nijinsky, except of course those who saw them, without those few penetrating frozen moments which are passed down to us? Duncan's rounded arms, Wigman's biting torso, Pavlova's legs, Nijinsky's rapturous indulgence. What distortions those words could create unless one could see for himself those rare arms, torso, legs, and flavor.

It is almost the responsibility of the artist to make sure his art is captured, somehow, for the future and for the future of the art. What would we all not give to see a film of Duncan dancing, the lack of which makes her stills so much treasured. Why didn't she insist on filming her dances? She could have: motion pictures were technically advanced. I can never forgive her for this oversight.

With the dancer the craving to see a likeness is not entirely the need of the ego. Dancers need to know what they look like when they perform; hearing or reading about themselves is not the same thing, because dancers look for different things. They look to see if all the things they slaved over in the studio are visible. They look to see if interpretation and quality have come through, as well as those secret things they had in mind which they will never confess to anyone.

The longest time I spend looking at myself during the day is while I'm shaving in the morning, although I must admit most of that time is spent watching the razor. When I next see myself is in the evening as I put my make-up on before a performance. The transformation created by those few pencil lines and the bit of liner I apply to my face always startles me. Someone else appears in the mirror. Someone else rises from that make-up table with a very different confidence and authority than the anxious performer who sat down ten minutes before. It's the eyes which change most. These new eyes clearly say "I know where I'm going."

I've had photographs taken of myself for twenty-five years, and I still ask myself, when I look at prints, "Is that me?" Why can't I recognize myself? Sometimes I'm amazed that others can. "Surely," some of my best friends confide to me, (while they also assure me that it is for my own good that they do so) "all performers are narcissists. All these photographs and all this displaying of yourself must mean something is going on between you and yourself." "Well," I think, "at least Narcissus recognized with whom he was infatuated." I never recognize myself, and anyway I get infatuated with photographs of other people, which I assure you is much more fun.

Making sense of photographs depends first upon how they are going to be used, from the candid gag shot, which one knows will be looked at with great amusement at first and cherished later, to the glossy Press Release shot reproduced by the hundreds and eventually stereotyped into an abstraction. The purpose of a photo is the clue to posing for them.

There are very few managers who will call a photo session for any other reason than publicity. Once the pictures are taken the selection follows a fairly predictable formula. 1. The clarity of the star's features. 2. Spectacle; the more acrobatic the better. 3. Anything against a white background. 4. A bit of acceptable flesh, and somewhere at the end of the list, 5. Quality.

"Look at the height of that leg," Tony, my manager will say. "But look at how the other leg rolled in," I answer, as I discard the photo.

"Look at that air shot," he'll rapturize, "Too much strain in the shoulders," I'll say, as another photo hits the dead file.

"What are you looking for?" he asks.

"I don't know," I confess.

"Christ, give me those pictures," he mumbles, "I'm looking for publicity shots and he's just looking."

For certain companies a photo call constitutes a performance; when that session is called onstage it means it is expensive. Chances are it is the only time that ballet will be recorded, and the fact that it will be performed by the original cast also makes it that much more important.

When dancers hear that there will be a photo call, they feel obliged to complain. In any case, they never fail to sound martyred. It's probably because they know the most knowing eye of all is going to watch them, the camera's eye, where passion cannot disguise bad placement. Dancing before a camera means you have to "put out." There is no óther way. When a dancer is being photographed a different chemistry infuses his blood stream. There is an urgency and push that goes a little bit further than the normal performing rush. It is almost as if he himself had to reach into the camera and sear his imprint onto the negative.

There are several kinds of photos one usually gets. Performing shots, which are alive and flavored with performing passion taken during a show, and those posed either on stage or in a studio, which usually immortalize the dancer's costume and teeth.

"A photographer is coming down today to take some shots during rehearsal. Just ignore him. He won't get in the way. We need them for the Sunday edition."

In the sixteenth century this bit of understatement might have sounded like "Oh we're sending an infected rat down this afternoon because we need some information on Plague victims. Just ignore him; he knows how to work with groups." Not that I am comparing a photographer with an infected rat in any way, it is just that there's no such thing as ignoring a photographer. As you talk, your arm gestures become broader, the angle of your head becomes adjusted, your glasses disappear, you've suddenly lost twenty pounds and your tights somehow fit. You're no longer standing in candy wrappers and old coffee cups and you stop squinting.

Posing for photos is a skill. Directing the best view of a movement toward the camera can become innate, with enough practice. When a performer senses the presence of a camera, he'll instinctively play to it, as he'll play to an audience once he feels their presence. Instant schizophrenia can be created by having a photographer appear in the wings while a dancer is directing his performance downstage. You can almost see them split their focus toward the two directions.

I never fail to chuckle when I remember the story of Anthony Tudor, Nikolais, and Oliver Smith who were seated together at a table as a photographer approached. Oliver Smith looked up and said, "My God if he takes a photograph of the three of us together we'll look like Mount Rushmore."

It's terrible how a magnificent performer capable of the most towering projection—secure, commanding, and authoritative— can be reduced to a bundle of anxiety before a camera. At a performance, the human eye, aside from being too slow to record every part of every movement, is also unreliable as to what it has seen and isn't particularly capable of still-shot recollection. But the camera's eye is ruthless, bitchy, and accurate. What is seen is what you get, and what you get is what you did.

A sloppy live performance can haunt you for a week if you're young and ten minutes if you're an old horse, but a photo of a bad performance is sure to stay around to line your grave and illustrate your biography. Probably the most chilling realization in dancing before a camera is that photos are evidence and as such create guilt. Now you see it, and now you still see it. They don't go away.

Next to an announced pregnancy, nothing can break up a rehearsal faster than the arrival of "contacts" from a previous day's photocall. Ego plays a role without a doubt, but the more important need is the craving which dancers have to see themselves. They must see photos to satisfy that need to know they are real, to know they exist, to know that the performance the night before actually took place.

This doubt that they are real compels them to see themselves in every way. Mirrors, store windows, photos, in print, anything that says, "This is you. This is you doing the thing you so painfully equipped yourself to do." But after each performance there comes the same doubts, the same questioning which only a photo can answer and assure. There I am. It was real. I really do exist, when all I had to make real to me that I performed last night is the muscular pain and the throbbing, things an audience would never know about or see. But there I am in this picture and that is who they saw . . . me, and for another day I do exist.

It's difficult to know when to trust a photographer. Some of them click away chortling enthusiastically, "Beautiful, perfect, great," and then deliver results which make you wonder if you should have learned how to type for a living after all. Or they come across like mice, looking as if they don't know how to load a camera, and then hand you a set of knockout prints two days later.

If there is any advice I can possibly offer to make a photo session more successful, it is to have someone sitting out front who sees what the camera is seeing—to check out grooming, costumes, camera angles and other little details which can turn a photo session from a bonanza into a blight. I remember one set of contacts where a skirt hem was prominantly emphasized by a long thread dangling from it. They were great shots in every other respect, but that lonely thread made them poignant and ludicrous as well as useless.

Someone should be out there to look for safety pins, dirty feet, throat strain, opened seams, and angles which reveal curvatures and deformities guaranteed to make the centerfold of the orthopedics monthly. For some crazy reason, photographers don't see these things. "Oh! I thought that is what you wanted."

Obviously a photograph can create an infinitely finer likeness than any other medium. But when it is taken by an artist, it can reveal character and charisma and offer clues as to what constitutes greatness in the personality of the subject. When a portrait is painted the personality of the painter often intrudes, and it becomes a portrait of the artist as well as of his model.

As far as I'm concerned, almost everything going for a photograph depends upon the photographer.

Art and publicity photography are two different things. The intent in one is to be enduring, the other to meet a deadline. Photographers are also very different people. Some can do still shots, some action. They all have different eyes for the right moment and different intuitions for when that moment is coming up.

In the back of the photographer's head there rests his consciousness of what certain art editors prefer. Art editors are not to be taken lightly. They should be included together with producers on everyone's list of necessary seductions.

At one time dance photos ran the range of a very narrow gamut. I remember one issue of a dance magazine, not too long ago, which had five different couples in five different stories all posed in the same position. But today dance press photography has become a great deal more adventuresome.

One of the reasons that dance shots fall into familiar and stereotyped composition is that the most exciting facet of dance is the motional, and the motional quality of a dancer is unfortunately almost impossible to capture in a clear still shot. Sports photographers do get great action shots, but then they have plenty of light on the courts or outdoors and the more anguished the look on the player's face, the more vital the action appears. Dance photographers are for the most part limited to the available stage light, and anguish doesn't sell tickets. Characterizations and strongly sculptured sequences have a much better time of it, because the choreographer is obviously calling attention to shape and detail and allows time for them to register in the audience's eye.

A savvy photographer knows how to frame a shot in his viewer, giving the dancer sufficient space to breath, but there are still some who use the amputation technique to frame their shots. I always get the creeps when I look at pictures cut at the mid-thigh.

The best shots will come when the dancer knows his role fully, right down to the eyes and fingertips, because this fulfillment of gesture can breath eternal life into a frozen moment. The thrust of the neck or the strength in the lower spine make a movement live on stage as it will in a photograph.

Inevitably there is the press photo to accompany an interview. On the road a little plump man will appear with a scrubby scrap of paper in his hand. "You're Murray Louis," he'll read.

"Yes."

"I'm supposed to get some shots of you showing some dancers how to do some steps." Usually you have just changed into street clothes and are on the way out of the theater.

"We've finished rehearsals about a half-hour ago," you explain, "and everyone has left."

"Can you find someone and do it here in the hallway?" he suggests.

Some dancers feel these conversations can cause cancer, others feel they reach so deeply they can cure it. Heart failure is another condition you can get from photo sessions, especially when you're seated in the back of the orchestra watching a photographer fussing to get his camera ready while the best shots are being performed.

Max Waldman and I play this game all the time.

Max: Murray, give me some good poses.

Murray: Okay Max, if you take some good snaps.

The best photos are often taken by one's memory. But there is one photo

I'm sorry was never taken by a camera. One morning at 2:00 A.M., after an opening night reception, I found myself together with Nureyev and Bette Midler sitting on three garbage cans outside of the restaurant "21" waiting for a cab. We were all loaded and singing, I believe, as we sank slowly into the cans and suddenly I thought, this is a picture I wish I had.

Istanbul

As I See It

I have always thought of dance as a language. A language that speaks through the human body. How clearly that language will speak depends upon how clearly the body can articulate; for I feel that with clearness of articulation there comes clearness of communication.

I have dedicated my life to dance and toward achieving this aesthetic clarity of motion. I have sought as a choreographer to select and arrange movement in a manner that would bring my audiences into this motional world, to evoke images and sensations, and by so doing, serve as a link between the outer physical world and the spiritual realm within.

Verbal definitions seem inadequate for so profound a subject as art. I feel that only through experiencing art can we enter that vast gorgeous panorama of the soul, to delight and tremble in this world of the senses.

To do this, the dancer as an artist must undertake a particular training, a training which will strip him of his pedestrian limitations and prepare him to reveal the inner life through all the means which comprise the art of dancing.

Art is not nature. It is, however, man's way of making a new nature. Man does not have milleniums on earth to do his work as nature does. He is rushed through life all too quickly; consequently, he must create his beauty just as quickly.

Beauty is essential to the chemistry of inner fulfillment, and in order to complete himself before he passes on, mankind has, out of necessity, been urged to produce his own beauty artificially. It is at this point that the artist appears, and through the selection of materials and under the guidance of an inner judgment, he transforms these materials and creates a new nature, a man-made naturalism called art.

The artist-dancer transmits this new naturalism to the viewer with all the artistry he can muster, so that the audience can more readily absorb and digest this nourishment for the soul.

When I compose, perform, and teach, I work very directly from creation to performance to communication. This thread is fired by a passion, an urgency, and an immediacy called performance. Performance is the cauldron wherein magic, imagery, and the unknown are fused to intoxicate the senses of the audience. But before magic can be created, even the wisest sorcerer must consult his recipes. Once he has determined his ingredients, as with the greatest chefs, he throws the book away and creates, making new life appear where none existed before.

There are certain ingredients with which creators must be familiar. These are the principles which comprise the craft of their art. The dancer and choreographer must also acquire certain skills in order to reveal their art. The audience, too, must know their role before they can participate. They must come with open receptivity to what is placed before them.

The vocabulary of abstraction that the dancer and choreographer use begin with their instrument, *the body.* The body is, in a sense, an orchestra comprised of various instruments: arms, legs, head, and torso. They can be played in solo fashion or in various combinations. The dancer works very hard to develop the widest possible range of flexibility and expression in all of these parts.

The *space* surrounding the dancer becomes his canvas. He can draw upon it and define it in many ways. The space inside his body allows him to give texture and quality to movement. The *time* he employs can range from the pulse of the heart beat to the most exacting syncopations, to the denial of time altogether. The manner in which he *shapes* his body has the range and freedom that a sculptor employs. There are also *energy* and *dynamics,* and imbuing all of this is *kinetics,* the excitement which sends motional sensation directly into the viewer's neuro-muscular system.

All of these can be mixed in any fashion to allow the choreographer a new and different vocabulary for each dance.

The dancer, meanwhile, must learn and be able to perform all of these principles as well as develop other skills. *Motional transitions,* for example, are those miniscule attachments which join one movement to another which allow for the special piquancy a dancer brings to his role.

I communicate my dances through abstraction. I do not generally create story-ballets or interpret characters. In order to communicate these abstractions I use the language of motion, which I hope my audience can identify and read, not as a narrative but as a series of sensory stimulations.

In the art of dance, choreography must occur within a specific time, bounded by the curtain's rising and its fall. In addition, an abstractionist must use a nonverbal vocabulary that is not easy to grasp in one viewing. But what he does have, which is much envied by writers and painters, is that wonderful immediate contact with his audience: the live performance and the power inherent in that contact.

Constantly there is the question, "What is the purpose of art?" If I may paraphrase the question, I would ask, "Who is the purpose of art?"

For me that purpose is the audience, the public who in the large sense is mankind.

The choreographer creates the art and the performer communicates it to the public, but not in the public's own terms, because they already know their terms, and no new growth would evolve; instead communication exists in the terms of the artist who, hopefully, will lead them to new insights.

All living things need stimulants to grow. Stimulants for the senses are part of the artist's challenge.

Art is a stimulant for living and for life.

That is how I see it.

New York City